SPIN-FISHING FOR SEA TROUT

A Complete Guide to Tackle, Methods and Tactics

SPIN-FISHING FOR SEA TROUT

A Complete Guide to Tackle, Methods and Tactics

GARY WEBSTER

THE CROWOOD PRESS

First published in 2008 by
The Crowood Press Ltd
Ramsbury, Marlborough
Wiltshire SN8 2HR

www.crowood.com

British Library Cataloguing-in-Publication Data
A catalogue record for this book is available from the British Library.

ISBN 978 1 86126 987 4

Typeset by Jean Cussons Typesetting, Diss, Norfolk

Printed and bound in Singapore by Craft Print International Ltd

CONTENTS

ACKNOWLEDGEMENTS

I don't know how many of my fellow anglers I've stalked, disturbed and pestered for information over the years. Plenty anyway. You know who you are. And to all of you I owe both an apology – for your lost fishing time – and a sincere thanks for contributing to my education on sea-trouting and so to this book.

To the following fish biologists I'm grateful for their patient help on issues over my head, and for sending me off-prints of their articles: Dr Indigo Novales Flamarigue (Department of Biological Sciences, Simon Fraser University); Dr Robert S. Batty (Scottish Association of Marine Sciences, Dunstaffnge Marine Laboratory); Dr Craig W. Hawryshyn (Department of Sensory Biology, University of Victoria), Dr Deborah Stenkamp (University of Idaho); Dr Peter Wainwright (University of California at Davis).

I'm also grateful to the following experts for filling me in on coast-fishing tactics in their particular regions: Tord Andreasson; Mathias Ström; Steve Schweitzer; Jan Johansson; Martin Joergensen; Steen Ulnits and Claus Eriksen; and to James Kinnear for sharing his experience with fishing lochs.

Tommy Engström and Daniel Almgren of the Cykel och Fiske tackle shop (www.cykelochfiskecenter.se) have kept me hooked up to the local angling grapevine over the years and were also kind enough to give me the run-of-the-store for shooting some of the tackle photos appearing here. I'm indebted to them both. Thanks too to Jokke Kertulla of Kert's Fiskeskap (www.kertsfiske.se) for letting me rummage through his personal gear for lures to photograph.

Last, I'm forever grateful to my wife Maud and son Nils for giving me more line than any sea-trouter deserves, and for celebrating those days that I do come home with fish, and kindly overlooking all those that I don't.

1 INTRODUCTION

The sea trout is a relative newcomer to many parts of the world, including North America, where it goes by the name sea-run brown trout.[1] In its native Europe it has long been ranked right up there next to salmon as the premier freshwater game fish. There is no question that the sea trout has everything a sport angler could ask for: power, size, acrobatics and beauty. It's also one of the most challenging quarries you'll ever go after and, for my taste, the best eating of all!

This is a manual for spin-anglers who want to learn more about fishing for sea trout. There has already been a lot written for the fly-angler, but hardly anything for those who like to fish hardware.[2] This manual tries to remedy that. It covers what you should know about sea trout, as well as the tackle and tactics you'll need for taking them during different seasons and in different kinds of water, whether you're fishing on foot or from a boat.

How This Manual is Put Together

The information in this manual comes from a range of sources. Much of it I've taken from my own experience fishing sea trout on spin-tackle (about 150 rod-days each year). But I also borrowed a lot from the experiences of many other anglers I've known personally or through correspondence. Some fish hardware, some the fly, some bait. To fill the gaps, I culled the fishing literature for anything useful I could find about taking sea trout on spin-gear.

Most of this manual deals with how to choose the best combination of lures and presentations for taking sea trout under different conditions.

Chapter 2 goes into detail about what makes a good sea-trout lure. It's heavy on spoons because, in my experience, that's your best lure-choice under most circumstances. But it also covers spinners and crankbaits because there are times when fishing these lures can save the day.

Chapter 3 covers a number of different options for presenting a lure in currents and in still water. It describes the most effective ways to deliver a lure into the strike zone when casting, harling, trolling and fishing through the ice. It also describes the kinds of tackle and tackle set-ups that will let you do that, as well as how to play and land fish.

Some of the presentations described in Chapter 3 are common moves used by gear anglers for other kinds of trout and even for salmon, which also happen to work on sea trout. Others have been adopted from the fly-angler's repertory, others were borrowed from bait-angling. Still others are less orthodox. I can personally vouch for the effectiveness of most of them. Others I've included based on reliable reports, or because they seem to be worth a shot given what we know about sea trout.

Chapter 4 covers tactics. It describes how to think tactically and it gives recommendations on lures and presentations when fishing rivers, tailwaters, estuaries, coastlines and lakes. Bernie Taylor, author of *Big Trout*, pointed out that anglers would catch more fish if they fished only when the conditions were in their favour, like predators do. Can't argue with that. But most of us fish for sport, not survival. We want to fish, when we want to fish. For the hard-core sea-trouters I know (myself included) that's pretty much whenever we can. But that also means that most of the time we're fishing under conditions ranging from less-than-ideal to down-right bad. On top of that, we expect to catch something every time we go out! Reasonable? Probably not. But that's sport fishing. So, in Chapter 4 you'll find tactics that should work when conditions are good, along with tactics that should give you a decent chance of success when conditions are less than good, which is probably going to be most of the time.

Follow the guidelines laid out in Chapters 2, 3 and 4, and you should see improvement in your performance. But that's only a first step. Consistently successful sea-trouters are also flexible and innovative. They're able to adjust their methods to novel situations. In order to do that you need more than a set of recipes, even good ones. You need to understand why some lures and presentations work better than others. And for that you need a deeper understanding of your quarry. You need to know what make sea trout tick. So I've also included information on sea-trout physiology and behaviour, when it seems relevant. You'll also find notes at the end of the book that give a little more detail on certain points, along with links to the sources I used. All of my sources are listed in the Bibliography in case you want to follow them up yourself.

Meeting The Quarry: The Sea Trout

The sea trout, *Salmo trutta*, is a salmonid. This means it belongs to the salmon family along with all the salmon species, as well as other trout like the brown, rainbow, cutthroat and golden, and char like the brook, lake, Dolly Varden and bull trout, along with the arctic char.

Distribution
Sea trout are native to Europe and parts of Asia and are actually the migratory form of the more familiar European brown trout. In fact, biologists consider them the same species. It's in lifestyle that they differ. The sea trout is migratory, or what the Americans call sea-run.[3] The brown trout is not. Both are born in freshwater rivers and streams, but only the sea trout migrates to salt-water to feed and grow before returning to its natal river to spawn. Other trout species also have sea-run varieties including cutthroat, rainbow or steel-head, and brook trout or char. The sea trout is a sea-run brown trout.

Originally, sea trout ranged from the White Sea and Checshkaya Gulf of Russia in the north, throughout Scandinavia and the Baltic, west through the Faeroes, and Iceland and down the west coast of Europe from the British Isles south to northern Portugal. There are also some closely related migratory sub-species in the Black and Caspian Seas. But because sea trout have earned a reputation as superb game fish, they've been successfully introduced into many waters in North and South America, as well as Japan, India, Australia, New Zealand and parts of Africa. Along the eastern North American seaboard, sea trout now run up a number of coastal rivers from Newfoundland to New Jersey.

Anatomy
In terms of anatomy, sea trout and brown trout are nearly identical. In fact, when they are young it's impossible to tell them apart. But, once mature, the sea trout looks a lot less like a brown trout and a lot more like the Atlantic or Baltic salmon, *Salmo salar*. This isn't too surprising since they have very similar migratory life-styles and, at least in Europe, they are usually found in the same waters. In the British Isles and Scandinavia, for instance, it's very common to catch both on a single outing, which sometimes leads to confusion over which is which. But there are a few ways you can distinguish a sea trout from a salmon once you've got it in the net.

First, both sea trout and salmon are powerful, muscular fish built for a migratory life-style that can take them over long journeys including tough upstream migrations through fast, heavy water. Their high muscle density (more than 60 per cent of body mass) make them among the strongest freshwater swimmers and jumpers. A

A sea trout of about four pounds.

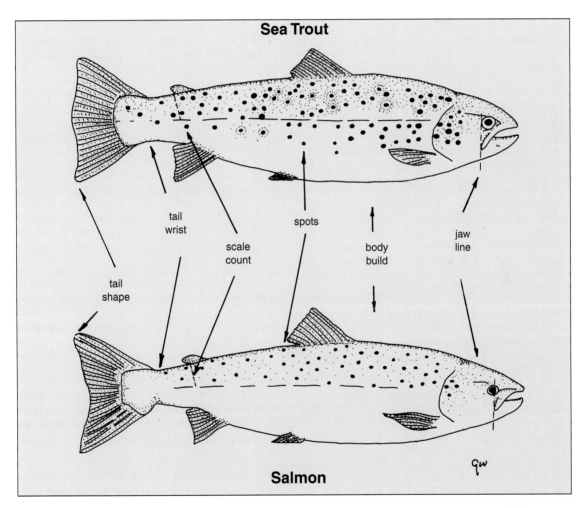

You can tell a sea trout from a salmon by looking at a few physical features. Body build: broader and stockier in sea trout than salmon; spots: larger and more below the lateral line in sea trout than salmon; tail wrist: thicker in sea trout than salmon; tail shape: square in mature sea trout, forked in salmon; upper jaw line: extends beyond eye in sea trout, not in salmon; scale count (along lateral line from rear of adipose fin to lateral line): thirteen to sixteen in sea trout, ten to twelve in salmon.

A salmon of about four pounds.

mature sea trout can swim up through a vertical waterfall a yard (1m) high, and can jump an even higher one! *Salmo* means 'leaper' in Latin.

A mature sea trout, however, usually has a broader, stockier build than a salmon, which is more slender and streamlined. Also, sea trout typically have more and larger spots than salmon, especially below the lateral line. Sea trout also have a much thicker tail wrist (caudal peduncle) than a salmon. You can easily land a salmon by simply grabbing it by the tail. Not a mature sea trout. Try that and it will probably slip through your fingers!

A sea trout's mouth is bigger too. This is easy to see if you look at how far back the upper jaw goes. On a salmon it just about reaches the eye. On a sea trout it goes back a little past the eye. The shape of the tail is also different. In the adult sea trout the caudal fins that make up the tail are about the same length so the tail looks more square. But the salmon's tail is always forked.

If you are still confused about the difference you can take a look at the scales. A sea trout's scales are smaller than a salmon's and there are more of them. So a sea trout feels smoother than a salmon of the same size. If you are still uncertain, you can count the number of scales running in a diagonal line between the rear of the adipose fin and the lateral line. The salmon will have between ten and twelve, usually eleven, while the sea trout will have between thirteen and sixteen, usually fourteen.

Knowing whether you've grassed a sea trout or a salmon isn't only insurance against embarrassment when bragging about it later. It can also be a legal issue. In most places the minimum taking-size is different for the two fish. In my area it's 15½in (40cm) for sea trout and 19½in (50cm) for salmon. So if my catch is under 19½in (50cm), I need to be sure it's a sea trout. Seasons can differ too. Where I fish, you can't take sea trout between 15 September and 15 October, but salmon are fair game. So I have to be sure which it is if I intend to take it home.

Basic Physiology

The basic physiology, and even much of the behaviour, of sea trout will be pretty familiar to trout and salmon anglers. Sea trout like other salmonids are high-performance fish with high oxygen needs. Since cold water holds more oxygen than warm, that's where you usually find them, in cold, clean, well-oxygenated water.

Now, the experts don't all agree on the precise best water temperature for brown or sea trout. But it is somewhere between 47 and 56°F (8 and 13°C). That's the range for optimal growth, feeding, activity levels and swimming performance. Sea trout can tolerate a much wider range of water temperature than that, from near freezing (32°F) to about 25°C (78°F), as long as they have time to adjust to it. But if water temperature varies too much outside the ideal range, both the trout's physiology (internal workings) and its behaviour will change in response.[4]

Sea trout like brown trout are also light intolerant or what is sometimes called phototropic. Part of this is probably because its eyes are more light-sensitive than most trout's. Part because the lower light gives them a greater sense of security and even some tactical advantages over their prey (more on this in Chapter 2). Because of this, the sea trout has earned a reputation for being an extremely shy and wary fish that shuns the light and seeks the security of shadows, structures and broken water.

Growth and Size

Many factors, including population genetics, determine how big sea trout grow. But one important factor is how salty the water is in the sea outside the sea trout's natal river, because that's where it will be spending much of its life feeding and growing. Unlike brown trout, sea trout develop salt-secreting cells in their gills when they are young. These allow them to regulate salt-balance (osmo-regulation) when in sea-water as cold as 40–47°F (4–8°C).[5]

Growth in sea-water is usually faster than in fresh: from 2 to 12in (5–30cm) in a single summer at sea, compared to 1½ to 3in (4–8cm) in a summer in freshwater.[6] Generally speaking, the saltier the sea the slower the growth. When the sea is brackish or not too salty, say up to 14promille,[7] osmo-regulation is easier and the sea trout can spend more time in the sea or estuary, where it has both salt and freshwater prey to feed on. When salt concentration is higher than that, sea trout must move into fresh or brackish water during the colder months where there is less to feed on.[8]

This means sea trout vary a lot in average size depending on location. In very salty (c. 30+promille) coastal areas like those off Norway, Ireland, Scotland, England and eastern North America, sea trout average about 2lb (1kg). In the more brackish Baltic (0–20promille), they are two or three times that heavy. For example, the famous Em in southern Sweden, which empties into the southern Baltic (c. 6promille), supports fish of around 13lb (6kg) on average. In Denmark they grow even bigger. Danish anglers report frequent catches over 20lb (9kg).[9] Large brackish bays in the Atlantic like Newfoundland's Spaniards Bay also grow big sea trout.[10]

Still, since some sea trout make long migrations away from natal waters to feed, very big fish are sometimes caught in typically small-fish waters. In Ireland, for example, where rod-caught sea trout rarely exceed a couple of pounds (1kg), the record catch is just over 16lb (7kg). The same goes for English waters where the record is 20lb (9kg)![11]

2 SEA-TROUT SPOONS AND OTHER SPIN-BAITS

No question, sea trout have been taken on every conceivable type of spin-bait. But of all of them, in my experience – and many sea-trouters will back me up here – it's the spoon that gives the gear-angler the best shot at hooking fish, day in and day out. Spoons are the first choice among professional tournament anglers; most of my sea trout over the years have come on spoons.

So why are spoons so great? Here are a few reasons...

First, spoons are extremely effective when it comes to triggering a sea trout's instinctive strike reflex. The strike reflex is deeply rooted in all predators. A sea trout is no different. It strikes at something because the movement, appearance, sound, even smell elicit a deep instinctive reaction. This natural reflex has been engrained through centuries of natural selection favouring fish that, when responding to certain sensory stimuli by striking, have often ended up with a mouthful of food! That's why if you put a spoon of a certain size, shape, action, colour and brightness in front of a sea trout, chances are it will nail it. Some writers have called this habit, some instinct. Whatever you call it, from the angler's point of view, the sea trout's strike reflex is its Achilles' heel.

This doesn't mean other factors don't come into play. One is the trout's equally honed anti-predator response: a spooked or wary fish may or may not flee, but it won't strike. Hunger is another – although not as critical as you might think. Clearly, an actively feeding fish will strike a lure more readily than one that is not. But even a non-feeding, spawning fish is a potential taker.[12] Spend a little time on a river where spawning trout or salmon are running, especially at dusk, and you'll see fish breaking the surface, sloshing in the shallows, even leaping into the air. Probably, many of these are striking at objects instinctively, not out of hunger or with any intention of actually eating them.[13] They are simply reacting instinctively to a well-known stimulus: a prey entering the strike zone. Remember: we aren't trying to get sea trout to eat our lures, only to strike them!

A second reason behind the spoon's effectiveness is how well it emulates the sea trout's favourite target: a vulnerable prey fish. All trout have a built-in attraction to prey that promise high returns for little effort. For the adult sea trout, more often than not that's a smaller fish. But not just any little fish, one thats behaviour indicates that it's vulnerable – in distress or wounded: one that promises an easy meal. That's what a spoon does better than other lures: it emulates an easy meal.

Finally, spoons allow greater control and versatility than other lures. It's simply easier to put a spoon where it needs to be under a wider range of conditions than other lures. You can fish spoons high, low, fast and slow, in heavy water and light. You can cast them short or long or right into the wind. You can present them effectively from the bank, or up to your waist in water. You can drift them, jig them or troll them behind a boat.

In this chapter, and throughout the rest of this manual, spoons will be given centre stage. That said, there are still some situations where a spoon isn't your best choice and other spin-baits can save the day. These lures fall into two groups: spinners and crankbaits (or plugs). I'll cover them too.

The Sea-Trout Spoon

What does a good sea-trout spoon look and act like?

First, it's important to understand that salmonids like sea trout have pretty poor vision compared to people. They can detect the relative size, and overall shape and colour pattern of things, but even close up, objects appear blurry. What salmonids can do extremely well is detect contrasts and movement. Anything that stands out against the background, and even remarkably small movements like the subtle wiggle of a meal worm, might elicit an instantaneous reaction.[14]

With this in mind, we can say that a spoon's (or any lure's) chances of getting taken by a sea trout are going to depend a lot on how it stands out and how it moves.

Let's look at movement or action first.

Spoon Action

A spoon's action is mainly a function of how it is built. Many anglers operate under the misapprehension that a spoon is a shiny, curved piece of metal that you attach a hook to. That's only partly right. Actually a spoon has two working parts: the body (that shiny piece of metal); and the hook. Both parts are critical to the spoon's effectiveness as a lure, because they work together to achieve the spoon's characteristic fish-attracting action.

In fact, of the two parts it is really the hook that makes or breaks a spoon's success, for a couple of reasons. First, and maybe too obviously, it's the last and only contact point you have with the fish. A broken hook, a bent or too-dull hook, a too-small or too-large hook translates to no fish on the bank. Second, nine times out of ten, it is the hook that a pursuing sea trout strikes (more on this below). If a spoon is a minnow, then the hook is its tail. So a spoon has a body and a tail. Body first.

The spoon's body drives the action. By action I mean its life-like behaviour as it moves through the water. The hydrodynamics behind this are fairly complex. Simply put, a spoon's action comes from the opposing water pressures on the spoon body's irregular surfaces, along with the opposing forces or drag set up by the tail-hook.

All spoon bodies are essentially curved pieces of (usually) metal, convex on the bottom, concave on the top and curved along the axis in either a simple 'C' (sometimes called a 'J') or more commonly 'S' bend. However, the precise curvatures and the resulting actions vary widely among spoon types. These actions are typically referred to as wide, slow, tight, lively, rear-end, front-end, regular, irregular, darting, high action, low action and so on.

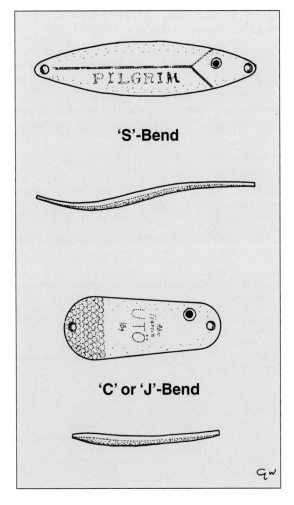

Spoon curvatures.

The spoon's action provides both a visual stimulus, as well as an auditory or sonic one by displacing water and sending out sound waves or vibrations, which are detected by the trout via its lateral line – that thin, dark line running down the side of the body at about mid-point. Sea trout use their lateral lines to detect prey, especially in turbid or coloured water.

Speed Limits

As with all spoons, sea-trout spoons have performance tolerances. That means they sustain their characteristic action within speed limits: too slow and there is little or no action, too fast and the spoon's desired action breaks into a spin. Generally speaking, the wider the body the slower the tolerances, the narrower the body the faster the tolerances. So, wider-bodied spoons work best in slower currents or at slower speeds, and narrower-bodied spoons in faster currents or at faster speeds. Narrow spoons also have less surface-resistance, so they sink faster for deep-water presentations, and they cast longer, especially important under windy coastal conditions.

Weight can also effect a spoon's speed tolerances. A heavier spoon will have higher speed tolerances than a lighter one of the same design.

You should be able to feel whether your spoon is working as it should. A throbbing pulsation – like a fast heart-beat – is the right action.

Sea-trout spoons come in a range of weights, and are usually classified as casting models in weights of from $\frac{1}{4}$ to $1\frac{3}{8}$oz (c. 7–40g) and as lighter, thinner bladed 'trolling' models or flutter-spoons down to $\frac{1}{16}$oz (c. 2g). Which weights you will need will depend on what kind of water you will be fishing and the range of presentations you're likely to be using.

Types of Sea-trout Spoons

You might catch a sea trout on almost any type of spoon. But when you look over the field of sea-trouting you find that the most consistently productive sea-trout spoons share certain features and can be grouped into three basic types: swimming spoons, drifting spoons and trolling spoons.

Classic Swimming Spoons: the Dart, Wiggle and Roll

This is the classic sea-trout spoon and the type of spoon that has probably accounted for most of the sea trout taken on spoons. First, unlike typical salmon or pike spoons, classic sea-trout spoons tend to be lenticular (willow-leaf) in body shape: pointed at both ends and widest near the middle. They are also deeply concave and have a fairly radical S-bend along the axis,

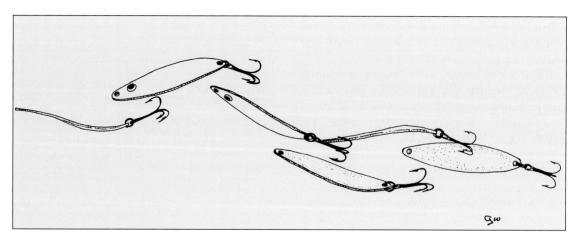

The dart-wiggle-and-roll action of a classic swimming spoon.

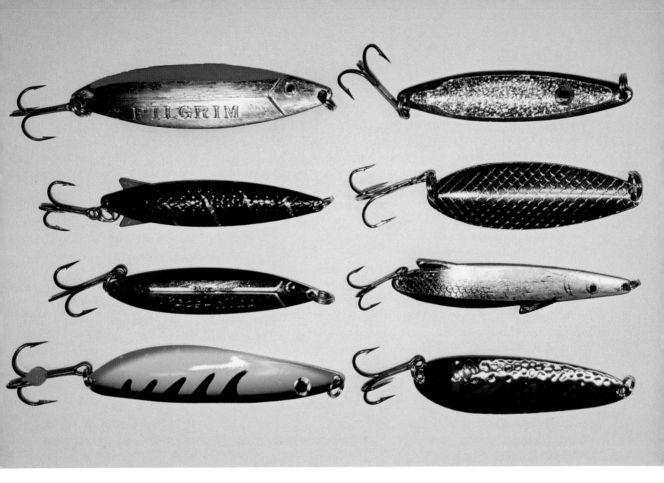

Classic swimming spoons.

with the larger or stronger of the curve in the front, and the smaller or weaker curve in the rear. This overall body shape, in conjunction with the tail hook, gives the sea-trout spoon a tight, front-end dominant, lively and irregular swimming action. I call it the 'dart, wiggle and roll'.

When viewed as a bait-fish impersonation, the classic sea-trout spoon's action combines a rendition of the wounded minnow with one of the distressed escaping minnow darting and rolling to avoid capture. That's why it is so effective at attracting strikes.

But its attractiveness is not without a cost. That highly erratic, irregular action also makes it a hard object for a sea trout to catch! That's not really surprising. Thanks to recent video studies it's clear that trout and salmon are pretty bad at capturing prey. They actually miss

a high percentage of the prey fish they go after. One reason is that prey fish can often out-manoeuvre them. One study by Raimchen showed that cutthroat trout lost about one of every three sticklebacks they struck at.[15] And video recordings by Dick Pool – a professional guide – documented even poorer performance by salmon.[16]

A high-action spoon is no different. That's why one of the most popular sea-trout spoons ever made, 'the Abu Toby', has a reputation for being an excellent attractor but a poor hooker. The Toby, with its erratic darting action, elicits plenty of strikes but often 'escapes' capture by a solid hook-up.

All high-action sea-trout spoons suffer the problem of poor hook-ups to some degree, but it's chronic for the larger size spoons because these tend to elicit a tail-stun strike rather than the all-in-one-bite strike that trout reserve for smaller fish (and spoons).[17] Typically, the striking fish is unable to get the entire treble of a larger spoon inside its mouth. The result is often an under-the-chin hook-up, or a single-point hook-up, which are sometimes thrown loose.

Over the years many solutions have been devised to deal with the poor hook-up problem. The great sea-trouter Hugh Falkus suggested taping or wiring the treble loosely to the tail of the body to dampen its wild action and provide the fish with an easier target. Another solution is to add a second split ring to the treble attachment. This also tames the wild tail action making it a little easier to seize, while at the same time making it more difficult for a hooked fish to lever the hook loose with the spoon body. Abu and some other spoon makers now double-ring some of their larger models.

Popular Swimming Spoons

- Jensen Sea Trout
- Mepps Syclops
- Gevo Laxi
- Luhr Jensen Coyote and Krokodile
- Landa Lukki
- Viking Herring and Iron Wiggler
- Hansen Thor, Flash, Karina, Fight, Pilgrim and Stripper
- Abu Salar (used only), Toby, Toby Rocket, Hammer, Sländan and Koster
- Filur
- Fläden Nidingen and Trutta
- Ron Thompson Slimline
- Blue Fox Möresilda and Candelfish

Drifting spoons.

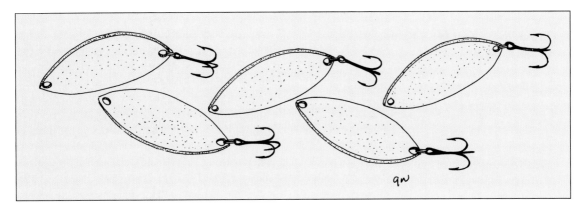

The hovering-wobble action of a drifting spoon.

Something that has worked for me is replacing the stock hook on larger spoons with one of smaller size (#4 for #2, #6 for #4). Then I add a small coloured bead (wire or yarn works also) to the shank. Because the smaller treble moves in a smaller radius, while the bead provides an easier target, a striking fish is more likely to end up with most or all of the treble inside its mouth and so it's less likely to throw it. The bead also adds enough drag to compensate for the smaller hook, so the spoon's action is less affected. Some spoons come with treble beads, plastic tail flippers, even fly dressings to draw attention to the spoon's tail as a target.

Plenty of companies make swimming spoons suited for sea trout (*see* box on previous page).

Drifting Spoons: the Hovering Wobble
Drifting spoons are wider, and less concave than swimming spoons. And the curvature along the axis is simpler – usually described as a 'C' or 'J' bend. These features make the drifting spoon a little more buoyant and also capable of maintaining what might be described as a 'hovering wobble' in still water or when drifting with the current. Some of the very earliest commercial spoons followed this design, such as Juleo Beul's original spoon-bowl spoon and the Pearl Wobbler popular during the 1920s.[18]

One of the first really successful drifting models for sea trout was the Abu Plankton,

which is unfortunately only available nowadays used. In contrast to the Toby, or Toby-like, classic swimming spoon, the Plankton, like other drifting spoons, as the name implies, isn't supposed to emulate a fleeing fish at all but something else, perhaps a small creature drifting helplessly in the current, like plankton do. There are plenty of commercial models to choose from (*see* box below).

Some Good Drifting Spoons

- Abu Plankton (used only), Salar (used only), Lill' Öring, Atom, Utö and Flamingo
- Bergen Spoon (Hugh Falkus' favourite, but now hard to find)
- Acme Little Cleo
- Atlantic and Whitewater spoons by Fishing Pool
- Gibbs Koho
- Dick Nite
- Blue Fox Pixee, Möreungen, Genial and Essox
- BC Steel by Pen Tac
- Eppinger Devle Dog and Red Eye
- Luhr Jensen Krokodile Stubby
- Johnson Silver Minnow Sprite
- Tomic

Tip: How to Double a Spoon's Weight

Here is a way to double the weight of a spoon without increasing its size. Simply sandwich two identical spoon bodies together by stringing both on the single set of split rings. The loose fit means they rattle and click when being fished but that only makes the spoon more attractive.

Flutter-Spoons

These are very thin and light spoons that weigh anywhere from $1/16$ to $1/2$oz (1.8–14g) and need extra weight to be cast or trolled effectively (*see* Ledger Rigs in Chapter 3). They are usually called trolling spoons or flutter-spoons. A lot of companies make flutter-spoons suited to sea-trout angling. Probably the most widely used in this part of the world are the Northern King models NK C5, NK 4D and NK 28. These weigh $c.1/2$oz (13–15g), and measure $2\frac{1}{2}$–$3\frac{3}{4}$in (4–10cm). Their best performance range is between $1\frac{1}{2}$ and $3\frac{1}{2}$mph (0.5–1.6m/s). Other popular models include Diamond King, Ismo King, Ismo Quack, Ismo Magnum, Pirate, Northern King Magnum, Iron Horn, Break Point and Big Horn.

Jigging Spoons

To the above three well-known sea-trout spoons, I want to add one more: the jigging spoon. Typically jigging spoons are thick compact slabs of metal somewhere between rectangular and lenticular in shape. They are also called slab spoons, blade baits, jigs, perks or pilks.

Unlike other spoons, jigging spoons are designed to sink fast and move vertically through the water with a sink-and-draw (jigging) motion, and to have an attractive action when they sink. They have little or no curvature and next to no action on a steady retrieve.

In my opinion, jigging spoons are not used nearly as much as they ought to for sea trout. Sea trout seem to find the sink-and-draw action nearly irresistible when these spoons are jigged either from bank or boat or through the ice in flowing and still waters. They can also double as a heavy-water swimming spoon. Because of their greater density and lower surface resistance, they are easier to work deep in strong currents, and to cast and control when it's windy. There is a wide range of commercially-made jigging spoons available. Or you can make your own (*see* boxes opposite).

Flutter-spoons.

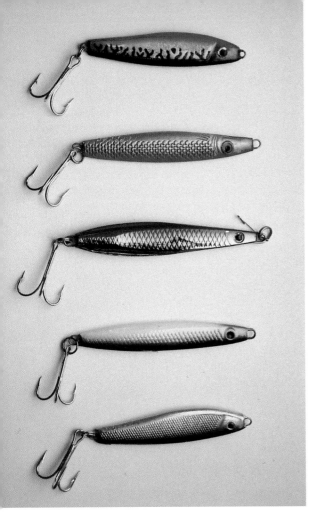

Jigging spoons.

Home-Made Jigging Spoons

Jigs made from the handles of common table knives are some of the most effective you'll ever fish, and almost too easy to make. You simply cut the handle from the knife blade with a hacksaw, drill holes at both ends, attach a treble to one and a split ring or two to the other, and you are ready to fish.

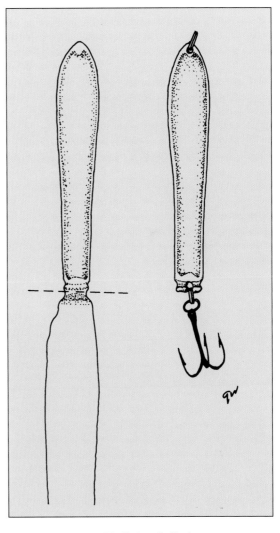

Making the fat-head knife-handle jigging spoon.

Popular Jigging Spoons

- Bay de Loc Swedish Pimple
- Nils Master Jig
- Luhr Jensen Crippled Herring and Needlefish
- Acme Kastmaster
- Fläden Öring
- Abu Krill
- Normark Vänern
- Twin Eagle Svenne
- Ron Thompson Fazet, Phantom, Solvpilen and Bristling
- Jensen Pilken and Tobis
- Hopkins Rattle Snakie

A home-made fat-head jigging spoon.

One reason knife handles work so well as jigging spoons, is their density. A 4in (10cm) long silver-plate handle weighs around 1½oz (45g), one about 3¼in (8.5cm) long around 1¼oz (35g) (steel is a little lighter). So these lures sink quickly and stay down when you want them to. A second reason is shape. You can make serviceable jigs out of almost any knife, even some spoon or fork handles. But the best have certain features. Look for handles that are fat and narrow at the blade end, and wide and thin at the butt end. These have a slightly more erratic – and apparently more appealing – movement when jigged up and down. But to make the most of that fish-attracting action, you'll need to attach the hook to the fatter, narrower end and the line to the wider, thinner end. I call it 'fat-head'.

I've started using this lure as a sweeping spoon too for heavy-water (and wind) conditions. But then I turn it around, hook the treble to the wider end, hammer a slight S-bend in it, and call it 'fat-tail'. So far, I'm real happy with the results.

On both I use a double-ringwire loop at the treble (#4 treble) end, which seems to prevent fish from leveraging the hook loose with the long spoon body. Sometimes I add a bead or piece of yarn to the tail hook as a target. Otherwise I fish it as is, in plain silver or with a little black or blue on it for contrast.

Some jigs are designed specifically for taking sea trout through the ice. Jigs like Abu Lurette and Bergan Pirk hang vertically on the line like normal spoons. Others hang horizontally on the line and have a tail fin that makes them run in erratic circles when worked up and down. Models like Rapala Balanspirk and Luhr-Jensen Ripple Tail have revolutionized ice-fishing on still waters.

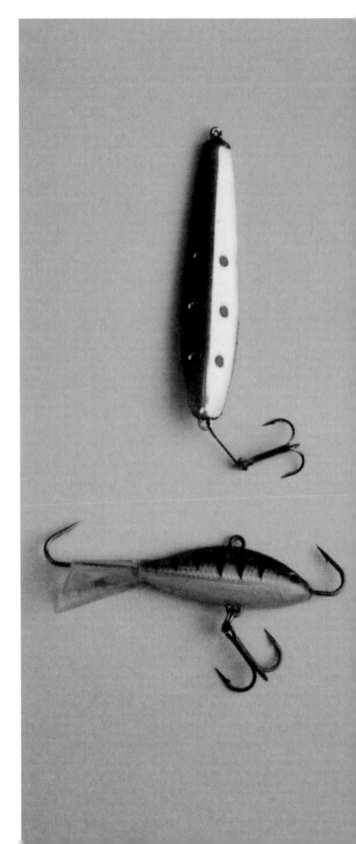

Jigs designed for ice-fishing.

A small percentage of sea trout – fewer that 10 per cent on most waters – will attain the size of this 30in (76cm) 8lb (3.6kg) lunker.

Spoon Sizes

We usually think in terms of a spoon's weight, which is important when controlling for depth. It also effects casting distance and is a critical factor in a spoon's action. But in terms of effectiveness, a spoon's size is just as important as its action.

Big Fish – Big Spoon/Small Fish – Small Spoon

One reason relates to how sea trout select prey. Once a trout reaches about 15½in (40cm) in length – the legal minimum taking size on many waters – its diet is almost exclusively small fish, with a preferred size of 2–4in (5–10cm). As a sea trout grows, it targets even larger prey. So a really big trout of 39in (100cm) will go for prey fish of 6in (15cm) size or larger![19]

Hugh Falkus suggested using spoon sizes of 1½–2⅓in (4–6cm); Harris and Morgan 1¾–2⅓in (4.5–6cm) and Jock Scott 1–2⅓in (3–6cm). Add another ¾in (2cm) for hooks and this is a range of 2–3in (5–8cm) overall. These are a little too small for trophy fish, but just about right for fish around 15½in (40cm). This doesn't mean that you can't catch trophies on small spoons, or that you won't hook undersized fish on large ones, but by choosing spoons with an eye on length, as well as weight, you can better your chances of taking the size of fish you are interested in.

So, who in their right mind would aim at smaller fish at the expense of taking a trophy? Well, plenty of anglers – myself included. First, targeting smaller legal-size fish in the 15½–23in

(40–60cm) range increases your chances of taking fish at all. That's because on almost any stretch of water these fish will greatly outnumber bigger fish by about three-to-one[20]. Besides, smaller fish fit in the oven easier!

Warm Water – Small Spoon/Cold Water –
Big Spoon

So trophy hunters should always use big spoons right? It's not that simple. Being cold blooded, a sea trout's metabolic rate is directly tied to water temperature. The warmer the water, the higher its metabolism and also its sensitivity to stimuli, like a lure. In cold water just the opposite: lower metabolism, lower sensitivity. So, a big spoon in warm water may spook rather than attract a keyed-up summer trout, while in cold water, it may take an even larger spoon to rouse interest.

Spoon Flash

Spoons are probably best known for their characteristic flash or brightness as they move through the water reflecting light off their shiny metal surfaces. The amount of flash, or reflectance, any spoon has depends on the kind of the metal it's made of and how it's finished, as well as on how much light is around to get reflected.

A ranking of the most common spoon body metals in decreasing order of flash would run roughly as follows: polished silver (most flash), plain chrome, matte silver, nickel, polished copper, gold, polished brass, copper, dull brass, dull copper (least flash). All have at times been effectively used for sea-trout spoons. But it is the silver-finish spoons that have gained a reputation as sea-trout killers.

Silver's special attraction for sea trout, especially those fresh in from the sea, is well-known among fly-anglers who have found success in traditional silver-bodied flies like Silver Stoat's Tail, Medicine, Alexandra, Sunk Lure, and others. This isn't surprising if you consider the importance to sea trout of silver-sided prey fish, especially during their long periods of feeding in the salt. Prey fish in those waters have developed highly reflective sides as camouflage

to help them blend into the clear watery background. When motionless they are hard for trout to see. It's when they flee, or swim irregularly when hurt or wounded, that the silver flash betrays them to a hunting sea trout. And this is just what the silver spoon emulates. That's why many sea-trouters (and steel-headers like Bill Herzog) swear by the plain silver spoon.

Cold Water – Bright Spoon/Warm Water –
Dull Spoon

But shiny silver has its limitations too. That bright flash that works so well triggering strikes in cold, clear, sunlit water is just as likely to spook potential takers when water temperatures and fish metabolism rise. Warmer fish need less flash to provoke a strike, so many spooners switch to duller metal finishes.

I know plenty of sea-trouters who fish nothing but plain metal spoons: bright ones when it's cold, dull ones when it's warm. And they do very well, in most situations. But for others, namely low light and turbid water, the shiny metal spoon can be improved with contrast or colour.

Spoon Colour

As in fly fishing, opinion on which colours work best for trout lures varies widely. Look at any lure catalogue and you'll find every colour in the rainbow. But little guidance about which work best, or when.

To start with, we do know that sea trout can detect the colour of things, even if the details are fuzzy. Like our own, a trout's eye contains both rods and cones. Cones to detect colours, rods to detect shades of grey. But whereas we do best with greens, they do best with blues and reds.

Among anglers this has led to two schools of thought: the colour-visibility school and the colour-stimulant school. Everybody adheres to the first. It is based on the sound understanding that different colours are more or less visible under varying conditions of light intensity and water clarity. So, trout, with highly developed colour acuity, should detect certain coloured spoons more easily that others under different light and turbidity levels.

Since fish almost always detect and pursue prey (or spoons) from below, the custom is to add colour (either paint or tape) to the bottom (convex) side of the spoon, since this spends most of its time facing down. The upper concave side is usually left plain in unfinished metal, i.e. silver, gold, brass or copper, so it can still flash reflective light from above.

Adjusting for Low Light
Sea trout's (and brown trout's) eyes contain a higher ratio of rods (light-sensitive) to cones (colour-sensitive) than other trout, which is one of the reasons they 'shun the light'. It also means they see much better than we do when light is low. In addition, they can adjust the rods and cones to suit changing conditions. During the day, the light-sensitive rods withdraw below the surface of the retina and are shielded by a dark pigment. At the same time, the colour-sensitive cones are extended upward for maximum colour sensitivity. Come dusk, the reverse happens: the cones withdraw and the rods protrude, giving the sea trout maximum sensitivity to contrasts in the grey scale. How quickly these changes occur is uncertain. Estimates range from several minutes to several hours.[21]

This all jibes well with anglers' experiences that the best times to take sea trout are usually at dusk, dawn or in cloudy weather. And this, as science now confirms, is when hunting trout gain a visual advantage over their prey.[22] To make the most of this, the spin-angler needs to use colours that are visible under reduced light conditions.

The mechanics behind colour visibility are fairly complex.[23] All the sea-trouter needs to know is that under diminished light intensity, long-wavelength colours fade and black-out quicker than short-wavelength colours. This is the order: red, orange, yellow, green, then blue. Red is least visible under low-light conditions, and blue most. So green and blue are good low-light choices.

Fishing deep water – even when it's clear – also calls for adjustments. Water filters out light. The effects on colour are the same. In clear water, red blacks out first, at about 15–20ft (4.5–6m) of depth, then orange at 30–40ft (9–12m), yellow at 60–70ft (18.5–21.5m) and blue at around 75ft (23m). Fluorescent shades of chartreuse, orange, red and green can be seen even deeper, down to 150ft (46m) or more.

Surprisingly, white is very visible under low light and in clear, deep water down to over 80ft (24.5m). And black is always black. So why not use a black and white lure all the time? Some do. And a silver-bodied spoon (which actually reflects bright white) with some black on the convex face is a very good sea-trout spoon. Moreover, the amount of brightness can be controlled by applying more or less black paint or tape to adjust for the trout's temperature-sensitive metabolism or 'spook' factor. It's an especially good choice for fishing in low light – even at night – when sea trout rely more on rod (black and white) vision, and the spoon's silhouette and contrast against a brighter sky are more important to detecting it than flash or colour.

Adjusting for Turbid Water
One reason sea-trout spoons are not all silver (or pearl or white) and black is because this combination is not always the most visible in off-coloured or turbid water. Much of our time angling for sea trout will be under less-than-clear-water conditions. But that can be to our advantage. Sea-trouters have long felt that the best water for daylight spinning is coloured or turbid. Graeme Harris and Moc Morgan summed up the consensus among the British sea-trouters in their book *Successful Sea Trout Angling* (p. 53):

Jock Scott, Falkus and Gammon rightly state that the best spinning water occurs as the flood peak passes and the water level begins to drop and starts to lose its load of silt and sediment so that it changes from a 'semi-opaque' appearance to the colour of 'pale lager beer or very weak coffee' – dependent upon whether the river drains an agricultural or moorland catchment.

In terms of visibility, that's roughly 3ft (1m);

clear enough, say, to see the toes of your boots when you're waist-high in water.

It's no coincidence that slightly coloured water is also what salmon and steel-head spooners also look for.[24] What's more, it turns out that scientists have observed a preference for feeding in turbid water among salmonids generally. Security seems to be the driving factor: even though fish can't detect prey as easily as in clear water, they feel less exposed and more secure when it's got some colour in it.[25] Some fish even switch from low-cost drift-feeding to high-cost hunting tactics when the water gets very dirty.[26]

Spin-anglers can take advantage of this by choosing lure colours that sea trout can see better in coloured water. But adjusting for turbidity can be tricky since it affects colour visibility differently than light does. Specific effects will depend on the colour of the water but generally speaking it is the reds, oranges and yellows, and especially the fluorescent hues of these colours, that remain most visible as water clarity decreases.[27] So these are going to be your best turbid-water colour choices.

Red and Blue

In addition to the visibility effects, some anglers – those of the colour-stimulant school – feel that certain colours, namely reds and blues, are more attractive to trout and more likely than other colours to provoke a strike. The evidence is both scientific and anecdotal.

First, it's now pretty well accepted that anadromous salmonids, like sea trout and salmon, shift colour-sensitivity seasonally. When at sea, their photoreceptors are blue-shifted, like most marine fish. Apparently this helps them in detecting prey in clear blue-green light-reflecting sea-waters. When in fresh or brackish water, colour sensitivity is red-shifted, similar to resident freshwater trout. This may help them detect prey in typically murkier freshwaters streams and rivers, where red is more visible.[28]

The results of lab experiments also add weight to the argument that trout like blue and red. One study by Ginetz and Larkin showed that rainbow trout preferred blue and could differentiate between a number of subtle shades. Second in preference was red (about ten times less sensitive).[29] Another study of cutthroat and Dolly Varden trout showed that reaction distance was greatest for red-sided prey.[30] And another by Semler showed that rainbows were more likely to attack sticklebacks with red throats than those without.[31]

Many anglers weigh in with similar evidence. Fly-fishing literature is full of references to the effectiveness of silver and blue patterns – many of which include a bit of red at the throat or tail – like Sunk Lure and Blue Night, especially for sea trout newly risen from the sea. Bernie Taylor, author of *Big Trout*, reports trouts' preference for trolled flies with red in them, and for red lures when ice-fishing.[32] Many spin-anglers like myself routinely use red as a target-colour near or on the tail-hook. And about 50 per cent of commercial spoons, by my count, feature some red or orange on them, regardless of the overall spoon colour.

So, blue and red: can't hurt, might just help.

Natural Colour Finishes

Playing the colour game doesn't have to mean spending a lot of time with paint or tape. Raw metal also reflects colour. Silver is really soft white, ash grey or lustrous white; chrome or nickel ranges from white to black; gold from deep yellow to amber; brass is golden yellow; and copper, soft red to reddish-brown. So even the natural-finish spoon purist can switch metals to suit both visibility and turbidity conditions.

Spoon Pattern

How colours or shades are put on the spoon is called 'pattern'. Some spooners feel it doesn't matter much as far as the spoon's effectiveness is concerned and believe that personal taste or aesthetics is as good a basis as any to choose a pattern. Others swear by certain patterns. There is some evidence that it probably matters to fish too, at least to the degree that certain patterns are more visible than others.

Simple spoon patterns that work.

Many spoons you find on the market today carry very life-like patterns. But, given what we know about trout vision, these probably aren't the best patterns for sea trout. As I noted at the start of this chapter, sea trout are extremely good at detecting contrasts, if not details. Some studies suggest they respond best to geometric patterns like stripes, bars, circles and spots.[33]

The problem with realistic patterns is that the shapes, colours and shades blend together at the expense of good pattern definition. It may look good to the angler, but it's probably not the best kind of pattern for catching the attention of a near-sighted sea trout. And remember, unlike flies, spin-baits are normally seen by the fish as rapidly fluttering objects. Any design with poor pattern definition to start is only going to appear even blurrier, and probably less attractive, when it's in action. For sea trout, simple two- or three-colour (or shade) patterns are probably your best bet. Don't overlook tradi-

Conventional spinners.

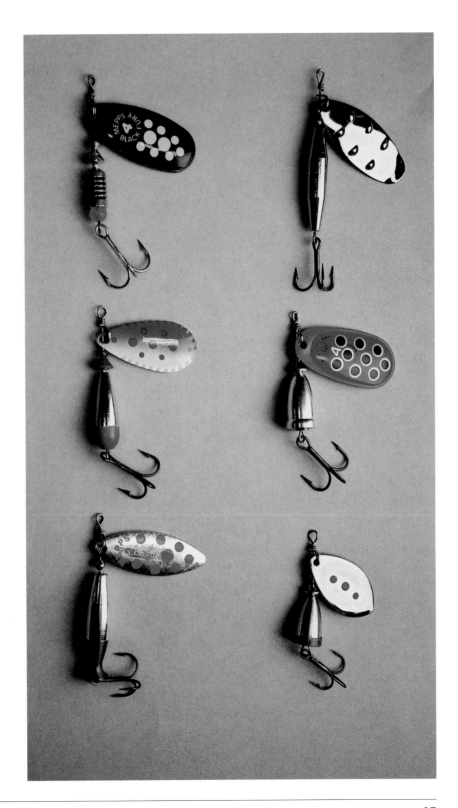

tional trout-spoon patterns like five-of-diamonds, daredevle (candy-cane), tiger, zebra, zigzag or simple stripes or dots. They're still around because they still work!

Other Spin-Baits

Now to take a look at some other spin-baits that will come in handy for special situations. First, it's mainly in action that these lures differ from spoons. Otherwise everything said about the importance of lure size, flash, colour and pattern still holds.

Spinners

It's easy to get confused when talking spinners. To some anglers, spinner means any lure you use with spinning tackle. It could be a spinner, a spoon or a plug. To others it means a lure that actually spins, whether or not you fish it with spinning or fly tackle. That's what I mean by spinner. Specifically, any lure that has a blade or fins or a body that revolves around a central shaft. The types that are usually used for sea trout fall into two categories: conventional spinners and minnows.

Conventional Spinners
Everybody is familiar with the conventional spinner. It features a central steel-wire shaft mounted with several metal or plastic beads or cylinders for weight, and a single (sometimes tandem) steel blade attached by a clevis so it spins when you pull in through the water, along with a single treble hook. The best known is probably the Mepps. This French-made spinner has been around for many years and probably accounts for more sea trout than any other single spinner.

For attracting fish, a spinner relies less on the flash than a spoon. Instead it counts on the flickering light reflections and high-frequency sound vibrations sent off by the whirling blade. Some models, like those in the Blue Fox Vibrax line, increase vibrations by including a special gear on the shaft. The spinner's vibrations make

it a very effective attractor when the water is coloured, since a fish can detect it coming via its lateral line even before it sees it.

Like spoons, spinners come in a range of weights, sizes, metals and finishes. Those most often used for sea trout range from sizes 0 to 4, which means 1–2in (3–4cm) long and $\frac{1}{16}$–$\frac{1}{3}$oz (2–9g) in weight. Most are single-bladed but some have tandem blades like the Hildebrandt Double-bladed or the EGB tandem. The shape of the blade also varies: oval and round-bladed models, like Mepps Aglia, Blue Fox Vibrax or Abu Droppen, are best for slower currents and speeds. Longer-bladed models, like Mepps Aglia Long and Blue Fox Deep Super Vibrax, are better for faster retrieves and currents. All the models can be had in silver, copper and gold finishes, and some manufacturers, like Mepps, Hildebrandt and the Swiss EGB, plate their blades with real silver or gold. Colour patterns, if any, are usually placed on the outside of the blade, sometimes on the shaft.

Many sea-trouters swear by these spinners for high fast-retrieves with the current (*see* Upstreaming in Chapter 3) because the light blade revolves (and attracts) even with very low water-resistance. In fact, a well-designed spinner can probably be counted on to work under a wider range of speeds than most spoons can. They also have less action than either spoons or plugs, so they tend to suffer less from poor hook-ups. Some anglers feel spinners are also less prone than spoons are to spook a keyed-up warm-water fish.

In theory, a spinner should be a great all-round lure but they have a weakness: they are hard to control. Once the blade 'catches' the water and starts spinning, the lure tends to 'take on a mind of its own' when it comes to direction and depth. Even the longer blade models are simply much more difficult to control 'in flight' than spoons are. I tend to reserve the spinner for upstream presentations, for light flows generally and for turbid water conditions. But more on this in Chapters 3 and 4.

One word of caution: spinners vary a lot in quality. Cheaper models don't spin as well at

The Flying 'C' spinner.

low speeds and sometimes stop altogether. It's always worth shelling out a little more to get the very best. Look for those made by companies like Mepps, Fishing Pool, Blue Fox, Abu, Hildebrandt, EGB, Double Loon, Panther Martin, Worden's or Sting King.

Right behind the Mepps spinner in popularity for sea trout (and salmon) is the Flying 'C' spinner. It's a little different than a Mepps-type spinner. First, the 'C' stands for condom and that pretty much describes the lure's salient feature. It consists of a long shaft of steel, lead, plastic or balsa wood covered with a rubber sheath – the 'condom' – which is flayed at the tail-end. It usually carries a treble, sometimes a single, hook and one or two spinner blades up at the head. The standard models are about 2–3in (5–8cm) long and weigh between ½ and ¾oz (12 and 25g). You fish these just like a convention spinner, but some anglers, and a few companies like Fishing Pool in the UK, are now making much lighter floating 'Cs' (about ¼oz or 7g in weight) that you fish off a ledger rig. Some fly-anglers are even making miniature 'featherweight' models suited to their gear.

The Flying 'C' comes in a range of colours and finishes, the 'condoms' are typically yellow, black, silver or purple, the blades silver or copper, sometimes painted.

As with other spinners, vibrations, which are probably enhanced by the 'C's rubber sheath construction, and blade-flicker are the main ingredients to its success on sea trout. Like some other spinners too, the 'C' needs to be 'kicked' into action to start the blade spinning with a quick snap of the wrist when working with the current.

The Flying 'C' seems to have come out of Ireland originally but now plenty of companies make them including Fishing Pool, Ron Thompson, even Mepps.

Minnows

The second bunch of sea-trout spinners, sometimes called 'minnows' includes Devons and similar lures like quills, and Irish or Lane minnows. Minnows are built differently than other spinners. They are essentially a tubular-body shell with two fins that spin around a wire axis or 'mount' attached to the treble. These don't have the flash of either a spoon or a

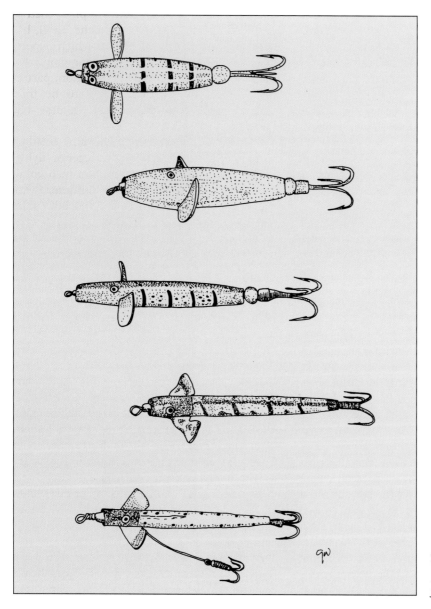

Minnows: (from top to bottom) *Devon, 'Severn', Irish, quill, quill with flying treble.*

steel-bladed spinner, but they do have a subtle little wiggle that, along with the vibrations set up by the whirling blades, seem to attract a lot of strikes.

I'll admit I don't fish these myself. But they've been a favourite among sea-trouters in the British Isles since the nineteenth century.

DEVONS

Of the minnows, Devons are the most widely used and, along with Mepps and Flying 'C's, probably account for most of the sea trout taken on spinners in the UK. Devon bodies can be made of metal, including lead, or wood, or plastic. The heavier steel models are fished much like a conventional steel spinner but it's the lighter, more buoyant models that have special value for the sea-trouter. The beauty of these is you can fish them off a ledger rig tight along a snaggy bottom very slowly – even motionless in the current – without hanging up (see Roll-Ledgering and Ledger Rigs in Chapter 3)

Body shape can also vary between long and slender, 'bull nosed' and fat-bodied 'Severn' models. Some models have flat sides, called 'Sprats', which give off a bit more flash than most. They can be had in almost any colour and a range of patterns. The most popular sizes for sea trout range between 1 and 3in (3–8cm).

Devons are also very good hookers and holders of fish. Like conventional spinners they don't have much lateral action, so fish have an easier time grabbing them securely. Also, they can't be levered-off as easily as some spoons can. Once a fish is on, the shell body slides up the leader and the hooked fish is left to fight the treble alone.

Due to their popularity, lots of companies make Devons. Unfortunately quality isn't a given. Some don't spin reliably, some carry fins that break off easily, or get brittle with age or under very cold conditions. So, as with other spinners, it pays to buy only the very best.

If your fishing in the UK, you can find Devons in almost any tackle shop. If not, you'll need to turn to one of the big mail-order houses, like Fishing Pool in the UK, which makes high-quality Devons.

QUILLS

Quill minnows are similar to Devons only usually slimmer, smaller and lighter, which makes them a favourite lure for fishing high and fast with the current (see Upstreaming in Chapter 3). But they also fish well deep with a ledger set up.

Quill minnows, as the name implies, used to be made all out of a natural feather quill, but now they are mostly of plastic, which experts like Harris and Morgan feel has only improved them. Apart from action and vibration, part of their appeal to sea trout seems to be their characteristic semi-transparent, minnow-like body.

Traditionally these little lures came bristling with hooks: one tail and two outrigger or 'flying' trebles. But most anglers fish them with either the tail treble alone or with one additional flying treble, which gives the quill a provocative side-shimmy action. Some experienced quill spinners like Peter Jarrams feel the stock hooks are too small for solid hook-ups and they replace the tail treble with one size larger.

You'll need to work a bit harder to find quills, especially from outside the UK, but you can get high quality handmade and painted models through the internet (www.FlyShack.co.uk).

IRISH OR LANE MINNOWS

These look a lot like quills minus the flying trebles and with a little extra weight. The body is wood or translucent plastic and you fish them about like a conventional spinner or a Devon. The Lane family out of Feale, Ireland, have been making the original 'Lane minnow' since 1949 and you can still buy them direct (www.laneminnow.com). Now other companies make copies called 'Irish minnows', which may or may not be as good.

Crankbaits or Plugs

There are lots of different kinds of crankbaits out there. Most are buoyant or semi-buoyant lures with fat plug-shaped bodies – hence their more common name 'plug'. Originally plugs were all made of balsa wood, now most are moulded plastic. As sea-trout lures plugs probably don't go back as far as other spin-baits. But today two types have become pretty popular: the Rapala-type diving plug and the coast wobbler. A couple of others (the Apex-type and wake lure) also have their enthusiasts.

Diving Plugs
Diving plugs have a bevel or lip at the front, so they dive down when being pulled through the water. By far the most widely used for sea trout are those made by Rapala. The original floating balsa-wood model, created in Finland by Lainu Rapala in the 1940s, is still a first choice. Other popular Rapala models include the X-Rap, Husky Jerk, and Team Esko – all floating – and

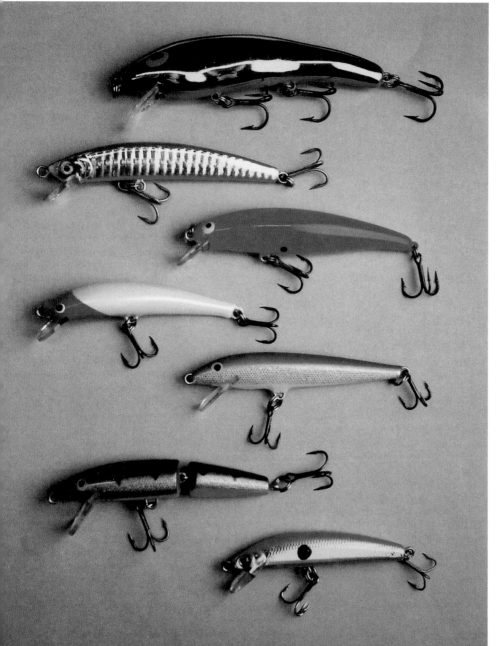

Diving plugs.

the slow-sinking Countdown. The Rapala original jointed model (2⅔in or 6.5cm), either in silver or gold with white belly, is a favourite for trolling on my local river.

Today you can get comparable-quality diving plugs from many companies, like Strike Pro, Nils Master, Bomber and Berkeley. Other favourites (especially in the UK) include the Kinnock Killer (or J-plug), Canadian Wiggler, Ace Minnow (Fishing Pool) and River Runt by Hedden (used only). I've also had good luck with 3in (8cm) Conrads (Fläden brand). The Kwikfish – a modern rendition of the old Helen Flatfish – is also worth a tumble when you're trolling.

As far as sizes, the most widely used for sea trout range from about 1 to 5½in (3–14cm) long. Most of these weigh between ¹⁄₁₆ and ½oz (1–2g) and so they are normally fished off a dropper-weight (*see* Ledger Rigs in Chapter 3). They come in all the colours of the rainbow, with lifelike fish patterns the norm. Unfortunately, many of these are too realistic and lack the fish-attracting qualities of good pattern definition and internal contrasts. You'll have to hunt around a little to find plain shiny metallic finishes. However, Coton Cordell out of Arkansas makes a line of plugs originally designed for bass and walley, which do come in plain metallic blue, silver and gold. The Rippin' Redfine model is gaining a reputation here for both sea trout and salmon. Yo-Zuri also makes the Crystal Minnow with highly reflective flanks.

A lot of sea-trouters swear by diving plugs, especially for trolling. They do have some clear advantages over other spin-baits under certain conditions: buoyancy is a big one. Like Devons, you can fish them deep with dropper-weights over a snaggy bottom without hanging up. Another is action. Most have a very active dart and wiggle action, which in Rapala's own words signals to a hunting fish 'I am in trouble'. These lures also tend to have higher speed limits than spoons, which makes them good for faster trolling speeds. Sound is another plus. Nearly every model nowadays is made with internal ball bearings that rattle and send out vibrations that sea trout seem to like. Lastly, they have good hooking power. It's simply hard to beat the two and three treble set-ups on these lures for hooking and holding fish.

So why use anything else? Plugs have a downside too. First, it's hard to get the fish-attracting flash of a silver spoon or spinner with even the highest gloss plug finishes. Second, plugs are pre-programmed to run at a specific depth range. Great for trolling, but less than great for other presentations that call for controlling and altering depth and speed. Third, while their action is reliable, it's also very regular and so lacks the erratic manoeuvres that make spoons so effective. Fourth, diving plugs are hi-tech lures with narrow design tolerances. That means only the best of them (the brand names) will work reliably, and those are going to set you back more than spinners or spoons – about twice as much. Here are running depths for some popular Rapala plugs:

original floating: 2–7ft (0.6–2.1m);

original floating jointed: 3–9ft (0.9–2.7m);

X-Rap: 4–8ft (1.2–2.5m);

Countdown: 2–12½ft (0.6–3.9m);

Husky Jerk: 4–8ft (1.2–2.5m);

Team Esko: 4–9ft (1.2–3.0m).

Coast Wobblers

These might be the only spin-baits designed specifically for taking sea trout. The story I heard was that spin-anglers in Gladsax, Sweden needed a plug they could fish very slowly in cold, shallow waters along the Baltic coast. The result was the Gladsax Kustvobbler. Now many other companies make coast wobblers too, e.g. Adexa VIC, Hingsten, Vicke, Kenetik Salty, Magic Minnow Sea Trout, Abu Tormenter Coast, Hansen Wims, Blue Fox Flutter, but it is still hard to find them outside Scandinavia.

As for looks, coast wobblers resemble other plugs except they carry only a single treble at the tail. Most are made out of solid plastic or

Coast wobblers.

epoxy, so they have a density somewhere between a metal spoon and a floating diving plug. And because they have no nose lip or bevel up front, they don't dive but run flat and have a very tight action. The most popular sizes are between 2⅓ and 3¾in (6–10cm) and weigh *c*.¼–¾oz (7–20g). They are thought to emulate one of the sea trout's favourite coastal prey fish, the sandeel or tobis.

Like I said, the beauty of the coast wobbler is that you can cast it into very shallow and near-still water and retrieve it very slowly along the bottom without hanging up. The long piliform body also casts well into the wind. This makes it an ideal cold-water lure, and it is a standard along the Baltic coast in winter.

Some companies have now started producing plastic coast wobbler–spoon hybrids, like the Abu Tanli, Rapala minnow spoon, Blue Fox Quiver and Blue Fox Dodge, but these don't seem to have caught on much among sea-trouters.

Apex-Types

These are a pretty recent invention. Although anybody who is familiar with the classic Helen Flatfish by Worden will get the idea behind them. They are basically pieces of flattish bent metal or, more commonly, plastic that have a very high-frequency dart-and-wiggling action when trolled.

These are rigged up a little differently than most other diving plugs too. The leader is threaded through the body, then tied to a small swivel attached to the hook. The body has two or three alternate hole placements for the leader, so you can alter the lure's action. Like other plugs they are usually run off ledger rigs (*see* Ledger Rigs in Chapter 3).

To be honest, I've never tried these lures myself but I've got friends who do pretty well, trolling estuaries with them. And they have become a big favourite among sea-trouters trolling deeper waters off Denmark's Jutland coast.[34] They come in different colours, but bright pearl white and green seem to be favourites in sizes 3–4½in (8–11.5cm).

Some models, like those by Sting King, even have small Echips embedded in them that send out electric charges to help attract fish.

Wake Lures

This is another lure I've only heard about, but, according to Graeme Harris and Moc Morgan, taking sea trout on wake lures goes back at least to the 1920s and 30s among fly-anglers in England's Lake District.[35] Because the method can be easily adapted to spin-gear, it's probably worth trying out in other places too.

Basically a wake lure is a small, floating plug bait you pull across the surface to make a V-shaped wake. It has no action itself. It's usually retrieved in smooth pulls or with jerks and pauses. The wake is the key. Apparently, when viewed from below the surface against a night sky, it is a deadly attractor. Wake lures are traditionally fished only in clear water and only on a dark night. Why wake lures work is uncertain. Some believe they emulate a drowning moth, others a swimming mouse, others a frog.

Hugh Falkus' Instructions for Constructing his Surface (or Wake) Lure

1. Trim a wine cork or cut and plug a goose quill for the body.
2. Tie up a tandem rig of two hooks with heavy monofilament as shown (something like a #4 treble and a number #2 single will do).
3. Whip the hook rig to the body with heavy thread and seal the lashings with varnish.
4. Fish it as is or paint the body silver, white, grey or black, and/or lash on goose feathers.
5. It should ride on the surface as shown with the single hook below.

The traditional wake lure has a short, fat body about 1½in (4cm) long made of either goose quill or cork. It has a big, single hook lashed (#1 or #2) underneath and a smaller

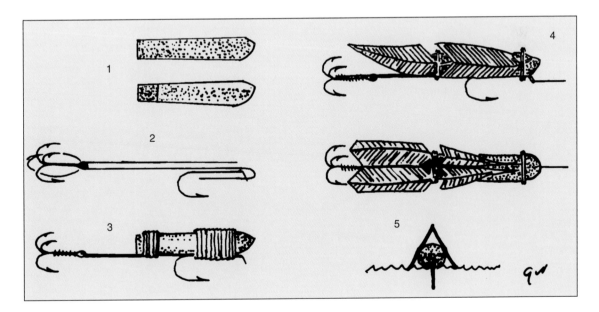

Steps for constructing Hugh Falkus' Surface Lure.

treble (#4 or #6) trailing behind. The whole thing is about 2–3in (5–8cm) long and weighs only *c.* 1/8oz (33.5g), so it floats.

Since these lures don't need to have action designed into them, they are easy to make, and most fly-anglers make their own. Because they are fished in darkness, when sea trout operate on black and white rod vision, any colour finish is pretty irrelevant. Most simply paint them black, white, grey or silver. Some also add a few goose feathers. If you want to give wake lures a try, you can make your own following Hugh Falkus' directions (*see* box on previous page).[36]

Or you can try using one of the modern surface plugs like a Rapala Skitter Pop or a Storm Rattlin' Chug Bug.

Adding Smell

It's pretty certain from research that sea trout use smell as well as sight and lateral line to detect and select prey. It stands to reason that a lure that smells like a meal, as well as looks like one, will be more effective than one that doesn't, especially in high and coloured water.

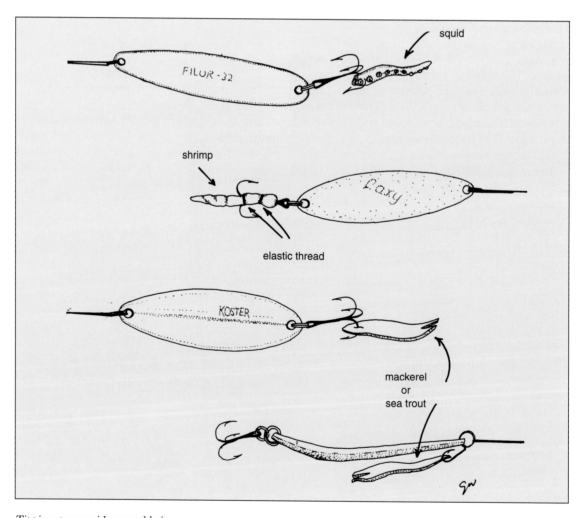

Tipping spoons with natural baits.

By all accounts sea trout have highly developed senses of taste and smell. After all that's how they find their way back to their natal spawning streams. Like other trout (and salmon) they've got nostrils and tongues, even taste buds inside their mouths and probably also outside on the fins and tail. But apart from navigation, it's hard to know just how much these senses come into play in detecting prey. Anglers using smelly dead baits like shrimp or squid often do well, which would argue that smell does matter. It makes sense that a sea trout is more likely to hold on to, rather than reject, a lure if it smells and tastes good. Or at least if it doesn't smell bad or alarming (*see* Using Stealth in Chapter 3).

There is a long tradition in sea-trouting of tipping a spoon's or spinner's hook with bait – in the British Isles, strips of mackerel or even sea trout belly are used, while in the Baltic, it's squid, sometimes shrimp. I have given them all a try at times. Personally, I can't report enough improvement worth the fuss (and mess) involved, but many anglers report good results.

There is also a wide range of artificial baits. They come in natural shapes, from worms to crawfish, as well as pastes and juice, and are usually called powerbaits.[37] They all smell pretty much the same – something like old shellfish – and some spooners report good results with these too.

Try tipping your lures if you are so inclined, but if you do, keep an eye on your lure's action when it's carrying bait. If you don't like what you see, try using a more lively spoon, or try attaching a small hook to the leading split ring (on the downward side) and impaling the bait on it. That way you still get the odour but with much less interference to the spoon's action.

Many rivers forbid the use of scents on lures, natural or otherwise, so check regulations first.

About Hooks

First is the issue of trebles verses singles. You hear a lot nowadays about anglers changing

Matching Single to Treble Hook Sizes	
Treble hook size	Single hook size
#2	#3/0
#4	#2/0
#6	#1 or #2

over to single, wide-bend Seawash hooks. They swear by them. They say they lose fewer fish and can release fish more easily without doing them undue harm.

As far as hooking quality, my experience is that trebles out-hook singles, and most sea-trouters I know use trebles. The little research I've seen on this question confirms the better hook-up rate with trebles over singles.[38] It may be that trebles do lose more fish once hooked than singles because the single hook often sets more deeply and can't be levered out as easily. But as far as safer returns with singles, I'm not so sure. Singles often sink very deep and make more life-threatening wounds than trebles.

About the only time I use singles is when I'm trolling spoons or spinners on an un-manned rod. I probably miss a few hook-ups I'd have had on trebles, but the singles seem to hold on to a hooked fish longer, which gives me the added few seconds I need to grab the rod and strike. If you are going to try singles, the round bend Siwash kind are best. And rigging up spoons, remember to connect it so it bends 'up', or toward the concave side of the spoon body.

So you've got a trade-off, more hook-ups and lost fish, verses fewer hook-ups and fewer lost fish. I opt for the first, because I learn a lot from hook-ups, even when I lose the fish. I want to know whether a retrieve and/or lure is working or not. The treble tells me more clearly when a fish has taken my offering – that's important.

What about sharpness? How sharp do hooks need to be? Certainly a really dull hook won't hold too many acrobatic sea trout. Compared to salmon and some other fish, sea trout have soft

Tip: Straighten 'Claw' Hook Points

Watch out for treble hooks with in-turned 'claw' points. These take a shallow hold and in my experience are too easily thrown by acrobatic sea trout.

If you are stuck with some, bend the point tips out straight with pliers before you use them. You'll lose fewer fish.

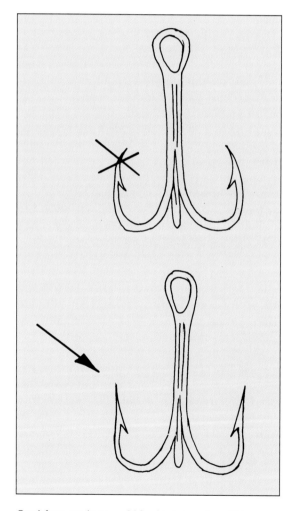

Straighten out in-turned 'claw' points and you'll lose fewer fish.

mouths, especially when fresh from the sea. Hugh Falkus went as far as recommending duller hooks for getting a better hold on fresh-from-the-sea fish because he felt overly sharp hooks caught on bone rather than finding softer flesh. Others like Harris and Morgan feel the sharper the hook the better. Some of it depends on how you fish. If you are fishing with the rod in your hand so you can react instantly to a strike, standard cut-point hooks are adequate. You don't need to spend a lot of money on super laser-sharpened varieties.

For most fishing, I prefer wire over cast-bronze hooks and a longer over shorter shank. Wire also lets me get free from a lot of bottom snags by putting steady pressure on the line and bending the hook out. Keep them sharp with a hook file or a whet stone and thrown hooks shouldn't be a problem.

Harling and Trolling can be different. You might have at least one rod in a holder or resting behind an oar lock and won't be able to respond as quickly to a take. In my experience a very high-quality super-sharp hook can make the difference on the free rod. It will often hold a fish that few seconds more you need to snatch up the rod and take control. The best hooks have cone sharpened points, e.g. VMC Needle Cone Vanadium, Gamakatsu Conical, Owner Super Needle, Eagle Claw Lazer Sharp Stingers, Mustad Chemical Sharpened. These will cost you though, about four times that of standard cut-point trebles.

Trebles also vary in flash and colour. Most anglers pay little attention to this detail, but some match the body with silver or gold or bronze, while others set up contrasts by painting them or adding coloured beads or yarn. Try each, if you have the inclination. As I said, my treatment is usually limited to affixing a target bead to the shank, usually red or orange, sometimes black or glo white.

Building a Tool-Kit

Now to put all we know about sea trout into

building a set of tools for catching them. We want a collection of lures that is varied enough in action, weight and size, flash/brightness, colour and pattern to cover all the situations we are likely to encounter on the water.

Spoons first.

Choosing Spoons

A complete tool-box will contain four types of spoons: flashy-pattern spoons; dull-pattern spoons; strong-pattern spoons; and all-rounds.

Flashy-Pattern Spoons

By 'flashy' I mean spoons that rely mainly on reflective light for contrast and brightness and so work best in clear well-lit water. You will want a few bright spoons for cold-water conditions. Real silver plate is hard to beat for its luminous sheen, but expensive. Chrome steel or polished nickel are much cheaper and work nearly as well. For warmer water, you will want a few not-so bright patterns. Gold plate is a favourite, but expensive. Polished copper or brass are probably just as effective and much cheaper. Added colour, if any, should be limited in coverage so not to cut down on reflective surfaces. Keep it simple: a stripe, a few dots of black, blue, green or red for added contrast is all you want. I also add a red or black bead to the treble-hook shank.

Dull-Pattern Spoons

By 'dull' spoons I mean spoon bodies with less glossy or matte finishes, which are often more visible under clear water, low-light conditions. For colder water, matte silver is outstanding in diminished light but pricey. Probably just as good and cheaper is pearl, or even painted pearl on nickel, which I use extensively. White paint is also good. For warm water low-light fishing especially at night you will also want to add some darker matte finishes, like tarnished brass or dull copper. Colour patterns can also help. Black, blue, neon blue, green, fluorescent green or glo white in stripe and/or dot patterns can be added for additional contrast. Shiny gold is good also if it's toned down with black, e.g. a

zebra pattern. I like to add a fluorescent red or orange, black or glo-white bead on the treble shank.

Strong-Pattern Spoons

In order to deal with the special challenges presented by very cold or ice-water conditions, as well as coloured or turbid-water conditions, you will need a few high-contrast, strongly coloured spoons. Silver or gold bodies carrying loud, garish patterns in fluorescent shades of pink, red, orange, yellow, chartreuse or green, with black accents for contrast, work well. So does black and white. Add a fluorescent coloured bead to the treble.

You will want to carry each of these patterns in both swimming and drifting models in small ($1\frac{3}{4}$–$2\frac{1}{3}$in or 4.5–6cm and c. $\frac{1}{8}$–$\frac{1}{3}$oz or 4–10g), medium ($2\frac{3}{4}$–3in or 7–8cm and $\frac{1}{2}$–$\frac{2}{3}$oz or 14–18g) and large ($3\frac{1}{2}$–$4\frac{3}{4}$in or 9–12cm and 1–$1\frac{3}{8}$oz or 28–40g) sizes. Add some thin-walled flutter-spoons in 3–$4\frac{3}{4}$in (8–12cm) sizes, and jigging spoons in the 1–$1\frac{3}{8}$oz (28–40g) weight range.

All-Round Spoons

There are at least a few good tactical reasons to have one spoon that you have good confidence in for covering most situations. One is the problem of new water. It takes time to learn which spoons work best. If you are only visiting, and haven't been able to tap into local expertise, you can waste a lot of time in trial and error, even when you've studied the conditions carefully. The same can happen on familiar water when light, water-level and even temperature are changing so quickly or unpredictably that you find you are spending more time changing spoons than fishing. Thirdly, there are always days when nothing in the prescribed arsenal works. These times call for a good all-round spoon. A good all-rounder allows you to keep a spoon in the water, to fish confidently and to think about more important things, like locating fish and getting the spoon to them – not to mention avoiding frostbit fingers on icy days! A good all-round spoon is designed to cover all

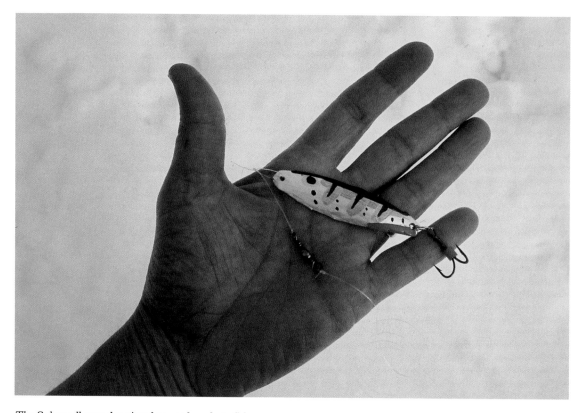

The Salmo all-rounder, rigged up and ready to fish.

the bases in terms of action, size, flash, colour and pattern. It might not be the absolute best solution in any given situation, but it makes a good showing in most of them.

After long experience most spooners hit on a favourite go-to spoon. For Hugh Falkus, it was a gold over silver Bergen or Norwegian spoon. For Jock Scott, the same in silver over copper. Many spooners where I fish go with something Toby-like in plain silver or copper. My own bread-and-butter spoon is a home-made creation I call Salmo (*see* box opposite). It combines the properties of a swimming spoon and a drifting spoon. It's painted in a stylized pearl, black and blue fish pattern that incorporates elements of some well-known sea-trout fly patterns, like Medicine, Sunk Lure, Alexandra and Marchog Glas (Blue Knight). If I had to choose one lure to use all the time it would be this one. I have fished it over entire seasons and under most water conditions and rarely felt like I was missing fish.

Choosing Spinners and Plugs

First, choose a few conventional spinners. Brand names only. These can be smaller sizes (#0 to #3) since you will be using them mainly for low-water situations – wider blade models for shallower flows, more elongated for deeper. I'd suggest one in bright silver (chrome or matte), one copper and one gold with garish or fluorescent colours. Add a few Flying 'C's also, both sinking and semi-buoyant in bright, dull and garish colours.

You might also throw in a few Devon, quill and Lane minnows to try, if you can find them.

Making the Salmo All-Rounder Spoon

Body length: 3in (8 cm).
Approx. body wt: 28g (1oz) in lead or tungsten sheet.
Treble: #4 (double wire-loop attachment or shank bead).

How to build the Salmo all-rounder:

1. Cut template of spoon body shape from stiff cardboard or plastic. Lay template on soft lead or tungsten metal sheet (c. $\frac{1}{16}$in or 2mm thick), trace with a scriber and cut out with wire snips. (Note: Lead is the easiest to find and the cheapest to buy. Try salvage operations and recycling plants. For a lead-free alternative, tungsten is non-toxic, and can be found in the same specific gravity (density) and similar malleability as lead, but it's harder to find and pricier.)
2. Drill holes (c. $\frac{1}{10}$in or 3mm diameter) at both ends of the blank for attaching hook and line.
3. Clamp the blank in a steel vice. Position it lengthwise and as close along the central axis as you can. You should see half of each hole protruding above the vice. This is important to ensure the spoon's lateral symmetry and ultimately that it has the action you want in the water.
4. With a hammer, bend the half protruding above the vice a little. You don't need to be too precise here. You are looking for something in the neighbourhood of 30–40 degrees off the vertical. But do make sure you have bent it all along the axis from hole to hole. The result should be a piece of metal with a crease running down the axis. This crease forms the concave side (the side that rides up) of your spoon body. Alternatively, you can squeeze the blank between two identical 1oz-weight Abu-Koster spoon bodies with pliers for the same crease.
5. Bend the blank lengthwise. You're going to do this by hand. You want to make a nice graceful S-curve with the longer bend toward the front and the smaller one to the rear. Precision isn't important because you can adjust the curvature easily at waterside if it doesn't run the way you want it to.
6. Prime inside and out, let dry, paint on Salmo pattern: pearl white on concave face, on convex face a black back, blue upper flank, pearl white lower flank with black dots, a yellow and black eye, and red-orange tail. Attach treble using loops of c. $\frac{2}{5}$in or 1mm-thick wire (copper, aluminium or steel). I use a #4 treble, either off a double-loop connection or with a soft plastic shank-bead in red-orange, black or glo white

Copying other spoons:

You can use the same procedure to make copies of any of your favourite spoons too. They work just as well and cost next to nothing. All you need is two identical spoon bodies. Use one as a template; squeeze the blank between both bodies to get the right curvatures. Paint it up; attach a hook (see step six above) and you're in business![39]

A note of caution:

Soft metal spoons have advantages and disadvantages. On the plus side is high density. They cast well, sink fast and have a good stable action. They are also easily tuned: the soft metal body can be quickly re-shaped by hand at waterside to get it running just right. Finally, they are cheap and easy to make. On the downside they are easily bent out of shape when being pulled loose from a snag, even when playing a heavy fish. Usually they can be bent back into shape by hand. Sometimes not. So, it's always a good idea to carry several backups. Take a badly bent spoon back to your shop, cut off the treble, and reshape it for another day.

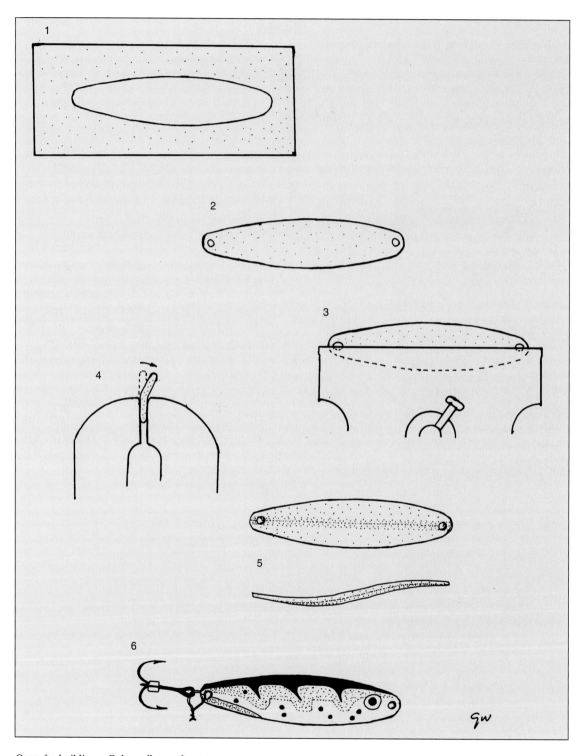

Steps for building a Salmo all-rounder spoon.

Floating models are most useful in small to larger sizes and, as in the other spinners, some bright, some dull and some garish.

As for plugs, you'll want a few floating-diving models. Rapala, Nils Master, Bomber, Strike Pro, Abu are all good choices. You want one with a bright pattern, like silver with blue, black or green back, one with a darker duller pattern like gold or copper with dark back, and one with a strong pattern in garish colours like fire tiger, or orange with black dots or stripes. Carry each in small (¾–2in or 2–5cm), medium (2¾–3½in or 7–9cm) and large (4¾–5½in or 12–14cm) sizes.

If you are going to be surf-casting, try to get hold of a few coast wobblers in the same sizes and patterns as your diving plugs.

Confidence

The first time I read *Sea Trout Fishing* by Hugh Falkus, I skimmed over the stuff about confidence. I didn't think it mattered: you use the right lure and the right presentation and you catch fish, or you don't. Attitude didn't get you sea trout, methods did. It seemed pretty simple. Well, I was new to the sport. Now I see what Falkus was saying: if you have confidence in your lure you'll fish it better, and you'll catch more fish. How right he was!

When I started out, I fished the local favourite – a silver and glitter-red spoon. I never much liked the looks of that lure. I still don't. I never fished it very well, so I never caught much on it either.

Now I rarely waste a second cast on a lure I'm not perfectly happy with. Even if a friend swears by it. If conditions call for a bright silvery spoon with some contrast, I buy one with a pattern that looks really good to me. Or I add a bit of paint or tape here and there until it does. Or I make my own. But I don't fish any lure until it says to me, 'I'm irresistible!'. If I believe my lure has a good shot at being taken by any fish it covers, I concentrate more on doing just that. I tune into water conditions more; I'm sensitized to every small vibration, throb, thump, ting, jerk or stop my lure makes as it moves through a presentation. I rarely waste a cast. Bottom line: I'm more efficient. And that means more fish per day!

Sea trout probably don't care this much about subtle differences in a lure's action or pattern, but I do. If it looks good to me, it fills me with the confidence I need to fish it the very best I can. That said, the next chapter deals with how best to do that.

3 HOW TO COVER, HOOK, PLAY AND LAND SEA TROUT

Chapter 2 looked at what makes a good sea-trout lure. That said, we have to face a hard reality: as far as numbers of fish in the net, it is probably more important how a lure is fished than what kind it is. If a fish can't detect or catch your lure it doesn't matter much if it's the best money can by. So this chapter describes a number of techniques for presenting a lure effectively in both moving and still waters, whether you're working on foot or from a boat, along with the kinds of tackle you'll need to do that. Most of these techniques are widely used for sea trout (and other trout and salmon). Some are less orthodox. I'll also discuss how best to set the hook, play the fish and get it landed.

First, some general guidelines on getting your lure where it needs to be – in the strike zone.

Covering Sea Trout: Putting Your Lure in the Strike Zone

The goal of any presentation is to cover fish. By covering a fish we mean putting a lure in the strike zone. It's what biologists call the trout's 'reaction distance': how close a prey or lure needs to be before a trout strikes at it. Recent research can teach us some important lessons about a trout's strike zone. The first lesson is that the prey (or a lure) needs to be a lot closer than you might think before a trout (or salmon) will react with a strike. For still water, the reaction distance is about 6ft (2m) tops, and for running water no more than about 3ft.[40] It's uncertain if a trout can actually detect a lure further out than that, but we know it won't strike at it until it's inside 6ft (2m). That's a small target to hit if you are going to cover a fish

effectively – and that's in clear water. As water colours-up, the strike zone gets smaller and so does your target. Newcombe was able to illustrate this by pooling a lot of published data on the relationship between water clarity and a trout's reaction distance.[41]

Take a look at the graph. It shows that in more or less clear water (less than 1NTU[42]), where the angler can see 10ft (3m) or more, a trout's reaction distance is just a little over 3ft (1m). But once the water colours up even a little bit (c. 7NTU), so angler-visibility is reduced to about 3ft (1m), i.e. those 'pale lager beer/very weak coffee' conditions we look for, a trout's reaction distance drops to about 2 ft (60cm)! And when the water is even dirtier, with less than 3ft (1m) of angler-visibility (c 20NTU), reaction distance is down to a strike zone of a foot (30cm) or less!

There is a another important lesson here too: it's that we can't trust our own eyes when it comes to judging the size of a sea-trout's strike zone! Just because we can see a yard (1m) or more through the water, it doesn't mean a near-sighted sea trout will strike a bait at that distance; its reaction distance will always be much less.

It probably doesn't matter much where in a sea trout's field of vision we place our lure. In front, to the side, above, below, anywhere except in the blind spot directly behind the fish, will do to provoke a strike, as long as it's close enough: inside the strike zone.

Getting the Right Lure-Speed

It is widely agreed that sea trout prefer a fast

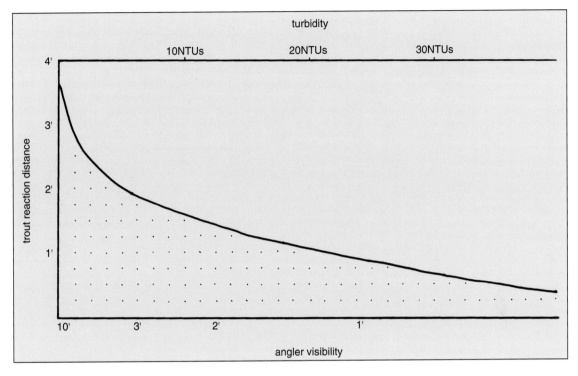

How turbidity effects reaction distance (after Newcombe 2003).

moving lure – faster, for example, than one fished for salmon. (The first sea trout I ever hooked nailed a spoon I was ripping loose with great force from a bottom snag.) So how fast is fast? First, a mature 15½in (40 cm) or larger sea trout has an attack or burst speed of around 10 to 12ft/s (c. 8mph or 3.5m/s) in ideal 47–56°F (8–13°C) water.[43] This is faster than its typical prey, like sticklebacks or sprats (c. 2½ft/s or 1m/s), herring (c. 5½ft/s or 1.5m/s) or even small trout (under 10ft/s or 3m/s).

Experienced trollers working still water, say speeds between 2 and 5ft/s (1½–3½mph or 0.5–1m/s) are the best for sea trout, depending on conditions. Now it's not too hard maintaining these speeds in a boat where you can watch the bank or use a speed indicator (*see* Harling and Still-Water Trolling below). But how about fishing on foot? Well, here is one way to get a feel for lure speed.

First, take your rod, let's say it's a nine-footer (270cm). Start by tossing out a lure into still water. Hold the rod nearly horizontal. Now, raise it up to twelve o'clock in one smooth action. It probably took you about one second to raise the rod from horizontal to vertical. If so, you accelerated the lure to a velocity of roughly 9ft/s (c. 6mph or 2.5m/s). That's faster than the recommended speed, but not too fast for a sea trout to catch easily.

Now that's in still water. When working a current you need to remember that the sea trout is already maintaining speed just to hold station, say about 3ft/s (1m/s). If you perform the same manoeuvre of raising the rod with the lure, fishing straight downstream against the current, you will be accelerating it at an overall velocity of about 12ft/s (3.5m/s). That's nearly 8mph! Too fast for a sea trout to easily catch.

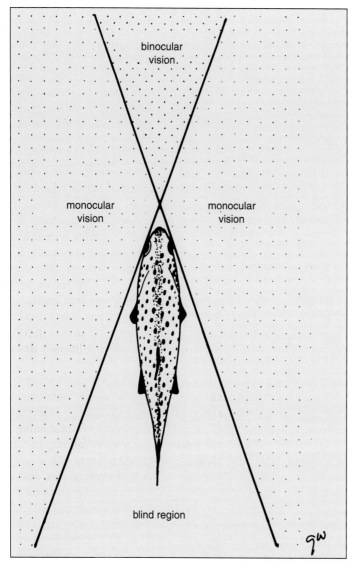

Trout's field of vision: trout only have good binocular vision and depth perception right in front of them. You can think of this area as a 30 degrees wide cone extending out from the nose. Then on either side of the head are wider windows of about 150 degrees each for monocular vision, but no depth perception. That's a total field of view covering about 330 degrees. There is also a blind spot right behind the tail, another cone of about 30 degrees.

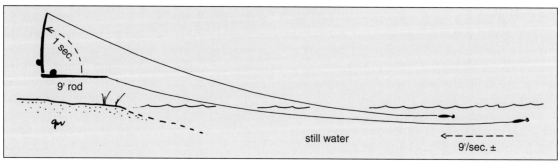

Estimating lure speed with the rod.

That doesn't mean you shouldn't ever move your lure that fast. Bursts of speed with intermittent pauses can be a very effective presentation: (*see* Drift-Jigging below). Sea trout are stimulated by the rapid escape manoeuvres of a minnow (or a lure) and will simply wait for it to pause before nailing it.

Cold water is another matter. A sea trout's burst speed drops by about half to around 5ft/s (*c*. 3½mph or 1.5m/s) when the water temperature sinks to 42°F (5°C) and the fish's metabolism slows.[44] That means in very cold water you need to slow the speed of your lure way down for the fish to have a shot at catching it. A useful motto: the colder the water, the slower the lure/the warmer the water, the faster the lure.

Coloured water also calls for a slower presentation. Remember, a sea trout's reaction distance is significantly reduced in turbid water – a strike zone of a couple of feet (60cm) at most! So you must make certain the lure stays within that smaller strike zone long enough to get taken. So another useful motto is: the clearer the water, the faster the lure/the dirtier the water, the slower the lure.

The same goes for reduced light. Lower light means less visibility for a sea trout and shorter reaction distances. So, slow it down: the lower the light, the slower the lure/the higher the light, the faster the lure.

Getting Your Lure to the Right Depth

How about depth? Most rivers are no more than 10–15ft (4.5–6m) deep, so practically speaking it's a choice between fishing deep or near the top, or both. Water temperature will be your determining factor. We know that in colder water, say below 47°F (8°C), sea trout will be less active due to slowed metabolism and will tend to hold and drift-feed near the bottom. At warmer temperatures they may be active throughout the water column. Our lures need to follow the fish! In deeper, still water, finding the right taking depth can be trickier. More on that below.

Presentations for Working Currents

The key to taking sea trout in rivers and tidal waters is learning to use the currents to cover as many fish as possible within a fairly limited stretch of water. Typically, this is water less than 15ft (4.5m) deep and 50yd (45m) or so across. There are a number of ways to do it effectively.

Drifting

Maybe the single most effective presentation you can master is drifting. This is where the wide-bodied drift spoon is unbeatable (*see* Chapter 2). Drifting works almost any time but is especially effective when the water is clear and cold. Under winter conditions, sea trout are least active, hold close to the bottom, feed very infrequently and won't move very far or very fast to secure a meal (*see* Winter River Tactics in Chapter 4) Still, few fish, even those nearly comatose from ice-water temperatures, can pass up a free meal, especially one that literally drifts into their open mouths.

That's what drifting is all about: delivering an easy meal. It's the spin-angler's version of nymph fishing. Only we aren't trying to imitate any particular larvae or pupa, just some anonymous, small creature drifting helplessly in the current. Maybe it's injured, maybe it's simply awash, tumbling along or hovering just above the bottom, wobbling, bouncing off rocks, momentarily fighting for control then losing it: easy pickings for a drift-feeding sea trout.

However, pulling off this presentation takes a lot of practice. Start by positioning yourself opposite the stretch of current you feel might hold fish. Now, you want to cast upstream far enough to get the spoon drifting along the bottom as it enters your targeted holding water. You want to do this with the lightest drifting spoon you can manage, since it is easier to keep it near the bottom without snagging, and because it will have good action even when drifting with the current. Just how light a spoon, will depend on current depth and strength, so you will need to experiment to get the best fit. You can also try adding weight (*see* Ledger Rigs

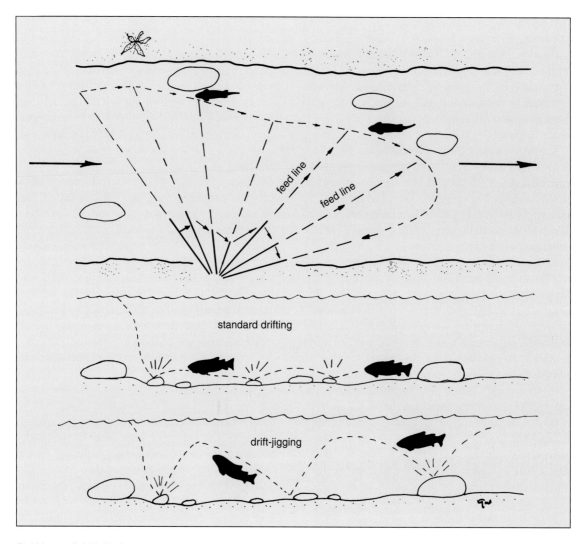

Drifting and drift-jigging.

below) but I find it hard to get a good controlled drift with extra weight on the line.

After casting, let the spoon sink until you feel it touch bottom. Then pull it up by raising the rod just enough to keep your spoon from snagging fast. The trick (and the challenge) is to keep the spoon drifting at that depth – within a foot (30cm) off bottom – for as long as possible. Let the current do all the work of carrying the spoon along.

You will need to adjust for depth throughout the drift, while keeping enough tension on the line to stay in contact with the spoon. Try to do this by only raising and lowering the rod if you can. Start at the top of the drift, with the tip low, and follow the spoon's course while raising it gradually as the spoon approaches opposite your position. As the spoon passes you, and begins downstream, you will feel it beginning to lift up against the current. Now you will need to counter this by dropping the rod tip again.

If you are drifting correctly you will feel the spoon tap the bottom every few seconds. Ideally, you won't need to work the reel at all but often it is necessary to reel in a bit of line at the top of the drift and pay out line toward the end. If you are using a casting reel, simply open the clutch and let the current take line. Or, open the reverse brake on your fixed-spoon reel and let the current drag out line. Some spooners advocate opening up the bale arm to feed line but this is a little risky, since you are out of contact with the spoon and have little chance of either detecting or reacting to a take.

Regardless of how well you pull the drift off, eventually the spoon will push up toward the surface and begin to swing around toward your bank. At this point you can decide on what kind of retrieval to use to get the spoon back home (*see* Hanging, Stop-and-Go and Bringing-it-Back-Home below).

If you worry that all the bottom-tapping will put off fish, don't. Actually it's one reason drifting is so effective. Well known steel-header Bill Herzog calls it 'ringing the dinner bell'. And that's about how it works in practice: by broadcasting the spoon's approach even before it comes into the trout's visual range and alerting it that something is doing just upstream, getting closer and maybe worth being ready for!

Drifting a little run. The rod is held high to keep the spoon fishing just off bottom at mid-course.

In my experience, sea trout will take the spoon anywhere along the drift. When one does, the spoon simply stops. Rarely is there a slam or jerk. So, staying in contact with the spoon at all times is important. When the spoon stops it's up to you to determine in a split second whether it's a fish or the bottom. Some say 'jerk or be one!' That's clearly the safest route. Personally, I like to feel it out a bit first before striking back. It helps to keep the spoon bobbing up and down just a little throughout the drift. Usually it's the up-bob that gets the hit: then I set the hook.

As I'll discuss below, it is much easier to drift effectively and to react to hits when using braid line, simply because it's more sensitive than monofilament. A longer rod is also a definite advantage when drifting (see Lines, Rods and Reels below).

Proper drifting is not easy but with time you will get the feel of your spoon's location in relation to the bottom. If you are snagging bottom a lot, you are on the right track. If not, your spoon is probably drifting too high. Don't worry about snagging, it's unavoidable. You can't drift properly and also guard against losing spoons to snags. As someone once said 'no lost spoons, no caught fish'. This is one good argument for making your own drifting spoons: less cost, less worry about loss, more confidence in playing it near the bottom (see Making the Salmo All-Rounder Spoon in Chapter 2). Unless you've got nerves of steel (or happen to be rich!) you'll find it's much easier mentally to keep a shilling's worth of spoon bouncing along the bottom than one that's set you back a couple of quid!

Tip: When Drifting in Unfamiliar Water

When drifting in unfamiliar water, especially when you can't see the bottom, start out with a lighter-weight drift spoon, then change to a heavier one until you're just grazing bottom. You'll lose fewer spoons that way.

Drift-Jigging

This is a variation on simple drifting that I like to use when the water warms up a little and fish are willing to pursue prey (and lures) more actively. It starts out the same as regular drifting with an upstream cast, but, instead of keeping the spoon drifting along the bottom, you step it down by jigging it with what is usually called a 'sink-and-draw' retrieve.

Drift-jigging is easier than regular drifting. Once the spoon touches bottom (or nearly bottom) raise the rod sharply to about 10 o'clock, then drop it back down a little more slowly until the spoon sinks down to near bottom again. Repeat this action all the way down the drift, feeding line as needed. Although this is a kind of drifting, swimming spoons and jigging spoons work best for drift-jigging because they sink faster and have a more attractive action on the up-surge than do drifting spoons.

Upstreaming

This is maybe the most effective presentation for sea trout in the summer when the water is clear and warmer, say above 50°F (10°C). In upstreaming the cast is made from well below the target water. The lure is retrieved high in the water – no deeper than a foot (30cm) below surface – and a little faster than the current, so the lure is back to your bank even before it gets too far downstream of your position. A small swimming spoon is the first choice for the job, a small spinner like a Mepps, Devon, quill, Irish or Lane a second. In clear low water it's always best to throw a good long line. If you need more distance add a little in-line weight. This is one of the only presentations that calls for actively working the reel's crank.

Many novice spinners find it hard to stick with this presentation very long simply because it seems unlikely a sea trout would grab anything moving that fast and high in the water. But believe me they do! And these are some of the most savage takes you're likely to experience. Often you will see the fish rocketing from the water with your lure in its mouth even

ABOVE: Upstreaming a small spinner in a run. BELOW: *Upstreaming.*

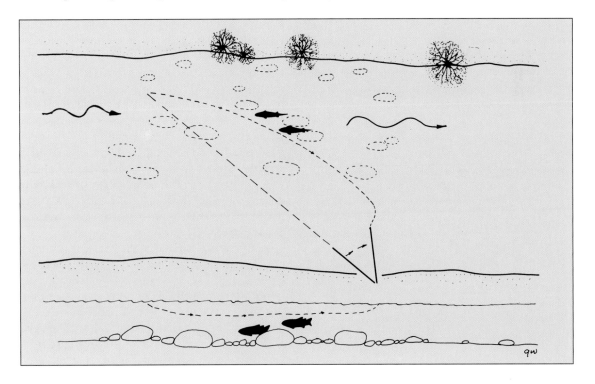

before you feel the hit. So, stay sharp and be ready to set the hook quickly.

Deep Sweeping

This is the classic over-and-down presentation. It's the bread-and-butter for many sea-trouters, as well as steel-head and salmon anglers. It allows you to work the lure high and low, fast and slow; to target specific lies or to work to a grid and it is effective under most water conditions (*see* Targeting versus Working-a-Grid below). My first choice for sweeping is a spoon: in normal flows a sweeping spoon, in heavier water a jigging spoon. But you can also sweep

other lures. In very turbid water a spinner can be effective. For working very cold water very slowly, ledgered flutter-spoons or minnows work well.

The sweep looks easier than it is and so you can waste a lot of precious water time if you don't do it right. This is a chronic beginner's problem: trying to learn by watching and copying what you think you see more experienced anglers doing. More often than not you get it all wrong. The novice chucks out the lure toward the opposite bank then begins to reel in slowly until the lure is back home. Effect? None on the fish. Maybe a sore crank hand after a couple of

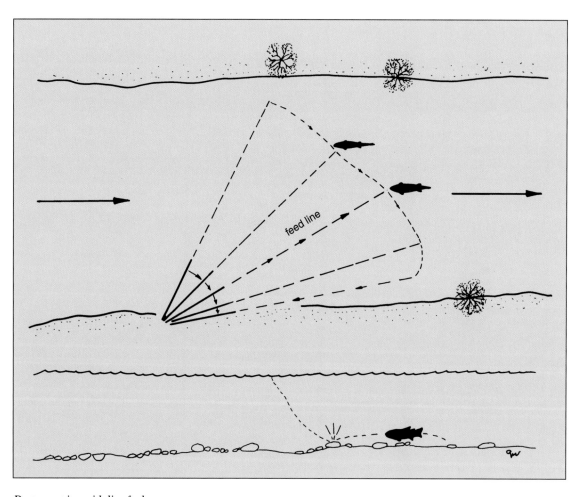

Deep sweeping with line feed.

hours and one dispirited angler. It's an easy mistake to make because it comes naturally. You cast and you wind and the current does the rest. The problem is the lure ends up riding at about mid-depth and about mid-speed: too high and too fast for a good cold-water presentation.

To sweep a lure properly, start by positioning yourself. Whether wading or working from the bank (or anchored boat) you will be fishing lies below you or downstream of your position. As in drifting, you want to get the lure to the right depth and speed before it enters your target water. Depending on current strength and depth this will mean casting somewhere between a little upstream and a little down-stream or straight across.

If the water is cold, you will want to get the lure down near bottom – inside a foot (30cm) – and keep it there, fishing slowly as it sweeps down and back to your bank in a wide arc. As in drifting, you'll need to let the lure tap bottom every few seconds so that you, and any potential takers, know just where it is. You can't worry about losing snagged lures and pull off a good deep sweep either. If it's a spoon, you should feel its pulsating action through your hands.

Unlike drifting and upstreaming, the lure will be working across and against the current the whole way. This means you will need to work a bit more at keeping it down near the bottom. You can do this in a number of ways. The first is by dropping the tip down from the start and following the lure's progress all the way around. If you need to hold the tip straight down in the water, do it. Sometimes when working shallower riffles, glides or pool tails, sinking the tip is enough to keep the lure just grazing bottom through the sweep. But when you are working deeper currents you will also need to feed line. As before, open the clutch or reverse break on your reel and let the current take line.

Mending a Sweep

Another trick for controlling lure depth, as well as its speed and path during a sweep, is mending line. This is basic stuff among fliers but seems to have come to spin-anglers through steel-headers

Sinking the rod tip is one way to keep your lure sweeping deeply.

like Bill Herzog. You can try mending while drifting also, but it is mainly when sweeping a lure that mending is needed.

The goal of mending is to keep a straight and more or less taught line between rod and lure. You do this by correcting the bow that naturally builds up in the line due to the force of the current by flipping it up and back – or 'mending' it. If you don't, the bow builds up drag against the current and pulls the lure up and around in an accelerated whiplash or S-course: not good.

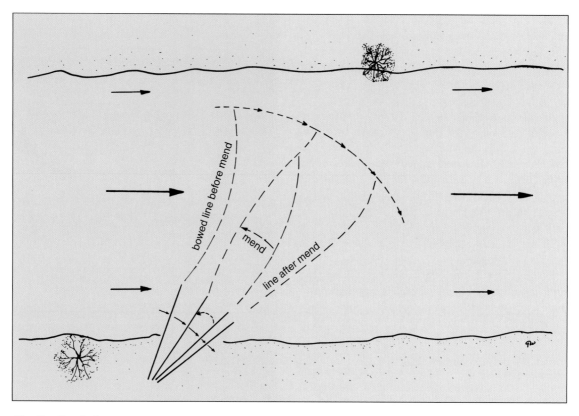

Mending line during a sweep.

How often you need to 'mend' will depend on the current. If you are working into a faster current, fewer mends will be needed during the sweep. But if you are working from or across faster into slower water – say you are positioned on the outside of a river's bend, for example – a bow will quickly develop and you will need to mend several times through the sweep. With practice, mending can be combined with line feeds and together used to keep your lure sweeping along the bottom, where it needs to be. If you are still having trouble keeping your lure down through the sweep, try adding weight to the line (*see* Ledger Rigs below).

You can also slow the presentation by casting a longer line and starting the sweep at a greater downstream angle. You will need to feed more line more often to keep the lure fishing deeply, but this is a good trick when the water is very cold or very dirty and fish need more time to react to your offering. This is also one of the few moves where monofilament line, which sinks, is a definite advantage over braid, which usually floats.

In my experience, fish will hit the spoon anywhere along the sweep, but most often as it swings around the bend. Because the fish will usually move to take the spoon, the strike will often be much harder than in a drift. In all the excitement, it's easy to forget to set the hook. Don't. Make certain you've got a solid hook-up by giving a sharp jerk, even if the rod is bent over double. You'll lose fewer fish.

ABOVE: *Mending line by flipping the bow upstream.* BELOW: *Sweeping a lure high in the water can be a good warm-water move.*

Jig-sweeping a home-made silver knife-handle spoon was the key to nailing this shiny three-pounder.

High Sweeping

This is a simple variation of standard deep-sweeping. It is the spin-angler's answer to wet fly-fishing. It allows you to work the lure high – in the top foot (30cm) of water – with variable speed. It is an effective presentation when the water is clear and warms up to over 50°F (10°C), especially at night when targeting shallow pool tails and glides.

The manoeuvre starts out like a normal deep sweep. Only in high sweeping you want to keep your rod tip up so the current can hold the lure just under the surface the whole way through

the sweep. To keep it there, as it begins to accelerate in the downstream arc, you may need to drop the rod tip, feed line or mend.

Alternatively, you can experiment by doing away with all line feed or mending and letting the lure rise and plane over the surface in its irregular path. You can also try high sweeping with a surface plug. I haven't tried this, but some report success with this rendition of the spin-angler's wake-lure fishing, especially at night. Jock Scott got his best results by 'jerky winding, say, two or three quick turns at a time, followed by a pause'.[45] As with upstreaming, expect hard, even acrobatic takes anywhere along the sweep.

Jig-Sweeping

This is the same as drift-jigging, only on a sweeping course. Like drift-jigging it's most effective under ideal water temperatures when fish are in top condition and willing to chase down fast baits. The best lure to use is a heavy jigging spoon.

Roll-Ledgering

Drifting, upstreaming and sweeping will let you cover fish under most conditions, but there are others that call for less orthodox presentations. These are mainly when the water is high and coloured with visibility of no more than a couple of feet (60cm), or in very cold sun-lit water when fish are holding deep in boulder-strewn runs or glides. Both situations present the same problem: how to keep a very slow-moving lure within a very small strike-zone long enough for a fish to take it. Roll-ledgering is the answer. It was originally devised by bait anglers as a way to fish light buoyant baits like shrimp, squid or worms very slowly along the bottom with the help of dropper-weights. But it's easily adapted to spinning.

In icy fast water the cast is made high in the glide and worked down, as in drifting. In dirty water, a simple sweep is carried out. But in both cases the bait is moved along at a speed slower than the current by allowing the weight to drag or hop along the bottom and act as a brake.

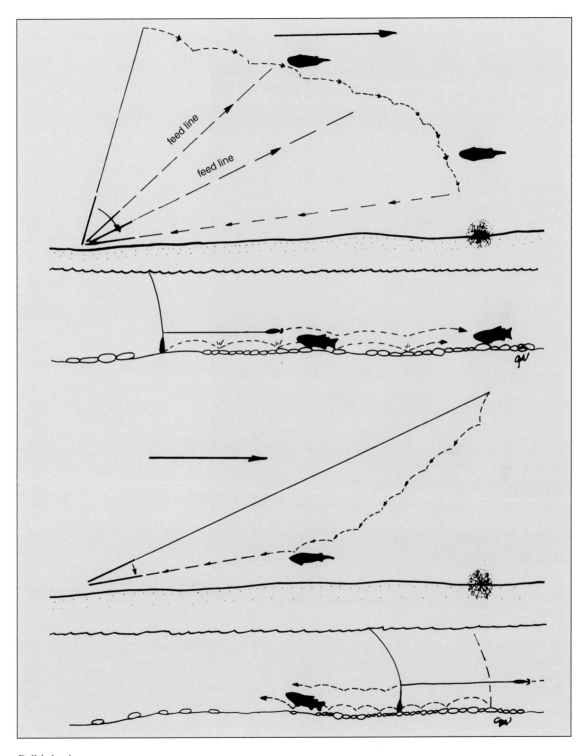

Roll-ledgering.

Dropper-weight and flutter spoon rigged for roll-ledgering.

That's the key. Breaking the lure's speed by dragging the weight along, while the much lighter lure is held just off bottom by the current.

You can't effectively roll-ledger casting spoons or conventional spinners; both are too heavy. But you can roll-ledger flutter-spoons, minnows, diving plugs or coast wobblers. My first choice is a flutter-spoon for its flash. Those

designed to perform at speeds of at least 2½mph (*c.* 1.2m/s) work best such as Northern King's C5, 4D and 28 models.

To roll ledger a lure, you need a dropper-weight set up (*see* Ledger Rigs below) but watch the leader length: too long and your lure will ride too high off the bottom. Start with about 2½ft (75cm) and adjust, if needed. You want to use a weight just heavy enough to bounce or be lightly dragged along the bottom by the strength of the current alone. You fish the ledger-rig just as you would an unweighted spoon, only it's the sinker, not the lure that keeps you in touch with the bottom. The sinker is your bottom feeler and speed indicator.

Just like a bait angler, you can vary the course of the lure and ledger: letting the current trundle the sinker across in an arc, or stepping it down and across by lifting the weight at intervals and feeding line, or stepping it up and across by lifting and taking in line at intervals. This way you can manoeuvre your lure in relation to structures or to better cover your target.

Backing-Down

This is essentially like roll-ledgering only you are working your ledgered lure – a flutter-spoon or a Devon work best – down a run from directly above it. This is especially effective for covering deep, fast boulder-strewn runs, when the water is either icy, even frozen (*see* Fishing Currents Through the Ice below) or very turbid. Both are situations where you need to keep your offering moving downstream very, very slowly and just off the bottom. Use the same roll-ledgering rig and adjust leader length and weight so you can back the lure slowly down the run. A long rod is helpful.

Falkus described backing-down with an unweighted diving plug (a Hedden River Runt) for warm-water salmon. It's probably worth a try for summer sea trout too!

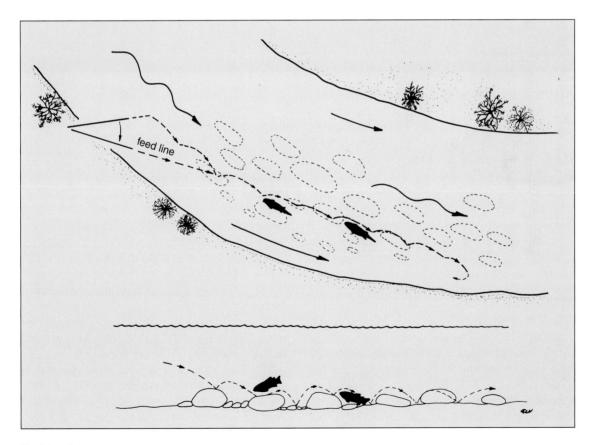

Backing-down.

Hanging a lure in the current.

Hanging, Stop-and-go and Bringing-it-Back-Home

Even the best presentations end. When they do, the lure is usually hanging straight down-current below you – or 'at-the-dangle', as they say in the British Isles. Now what? That depends a lot on what the lure was doing up to then. If it has been moving very slowly or even backwards, as in very cold or turbid-water situations, it can be effective to let it hang there motionless below you in the current, if that's possible. Fish will often take on-the-dangle under these conditions. In my experience, adding slight jigs to the hanging lure increases its attractiveness. (This is a favourite move in ice-fishing, *see* Fishing Currents Through the Ice below). Nobody can tell you how long you should let it hang there before reeling in and recasting. Patience seems to be the deciding factor. I have a hard time

hanging a lure for more than 10–15sec. I know a guy that seems to go into a trance hanging a lure for minutes. We both catch fish.

However, hanging isn't always effective and sometimes it is counter-productive. Following up a fast presentation under warmer conditions by letting the lure stall at the dangle can often stop a following fish in its tracks. It's more effective to follow up a fast presentation by keeping the lure moving at a good pace right around the turn and upstream back home. Often warm-water fish will take a fast-moving lure at your feet! I usually reel in from the dangle in stop-and-go surges: short and slow when its cold, or long and fast when its warmer.

Targeting verses Working-a-Grid

If you are lucky, you can mobilize the presentations I just described to target individual fish, or

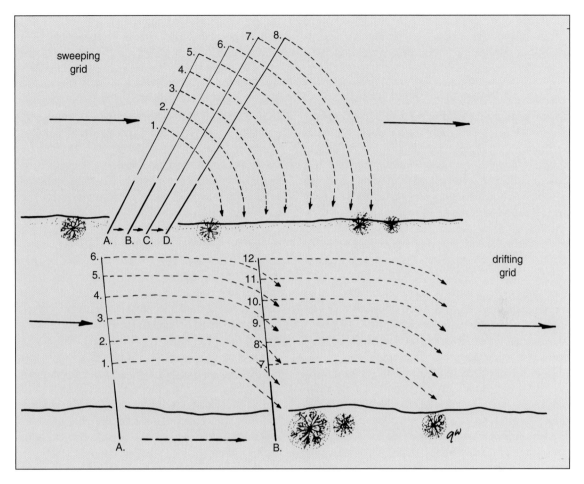

Grid-casting patterns.

shoals of fish, or specific likely holding spots, such as around stones or other structures. But more often than not, you will be fishing blind, without knowing precisely where fish are lying. Instead, you'll be targeting larger pieces of potential holding water, like a pool tail, a riffle, a glide or an entire section of river.

Under conditions when individual fish or specific lies are not visible or known, it is most efficient and productive to work the water systematically. The best way to do that is to visualize a grid across the intended water and to cast to that. Working to a grid is not only a more efficient way to cover holding water than random

casting is, it also helps avoid dragging line across fish before your lure can cover them.

You can fit any presentation to a grid system, but sweeping is by far the easiest. Work the near water first and start with short casts. As always, visualize the intended path of the lure and fish it out from start to finish. The trick is spacing. Make each cast a little further out and on the same line. I usually pick a target on the far bank and aim at that. Spacing should never be more than a sea trout's strike zone, so 3ft (1m) at the most. If the water is very coloured, less.

Once you've bitten off a sufficient width of the intended holding water – perhaps the entire width of a glide or pool tail, perhaps your half of a run – move down. If you are working a sweeping or upstreaming pattern, then again move no more than a few feet. If you've been drifting your lure, then move down enough to overlap the last set of drift paths. Once you've repositioned yourself, begin the casting pattern again. When sweeping or upstreaming you only need to make the longest cast, since you will have already covered the near water with your last cast. If drifting, simply repeat the whole pattern, making certain to overlap the grids. When fishing a grid, you don't need to spend much time on the retrieve, unless you feel you want to cover the near bank water repeatedly. Simply fish the first few feet or so of new water up from the dangle, then bring your lure home quickly. Working a grid can be boring business – it doesn't suit everybody's disposition. But if you stick to it, you can work every square yard (m²) of potential holding water, and feel fairly certain you have covered any fish present.

Before looking at harling and ice-fishing, one general pointer: fish out every cast. We all make bad casts – misjudging wind, current or depth, a finger caught on the line, whatever. But once the lure hits the water, fish it out as well as you can. It's time well spent. At the least you will learn more about the water and how your lure performs in it, at the best you'll get a surprise hit! Maybe even invent a new presentation!

Harling

Harling is essentially using a small boat to work currents. It's an old method of taking sea trout on larger rivers, but also for fishing glides and large pools in smaller rivers. Like bank presentations, you will be working your lure both with and against the current, as well as at different depths depending on the water.

Traditionally harling was done with a small, light, wooden row boat or dinghy, and it took two people: an oarsman and an angler. But today most us use a small boat fitted with a light outboard (and oars). This makes it much easier to work against stronger currents, and to keep your hands free to operate one, two or even three rods. Smaller dinghies of 10–15ft (3–5m) with 4 or 5hp outboards are typical on rivers where I fish.

At its most basic, harling is an extension of wading. You simply use your boat to better position yourself in relation to the holding water you want to target. The simplest move is to row or motor out, drop anchor and present your lure like you would when wading. It's an effective way to cover a river too wide to cover well on foot. It's especially effective when the water is very cold or turbid and you want to keep your lure fishing deep and slow.

Fishing from the bank you are always limited by the current pulling your lure out of its down-current path over toward the side. By working from a boat anchored directly above the target water, you can keep your lure drifting down-current almost indefinitely. Or you can sweep it back and forth, or back it down, or ledger it, or hang it in the current. Once you feel you've thoroughly covered the water in your casting range, you simple pull anchor, drift down to the next piece of holding water and start fishing again. More commonly though, harling involves trolling with or against current, along with downriver drifting, which is sometimes called back-trolling.

Like fishing on foot, harling is all about feel. You control the speed of your lure by controlling the speed of your boat relative to the current. You control its depth by keeping more or less in touch with the bottom. Since both river depth and current are changing all the time along any stretch of river, depth-sounders and speed-indicators aren't nearly as helpful as they are for still-water trolling (see Still-Water Trolling below). So experience and practice are the keys to harling success.

Up-and Down-Current Trolling

Trolling currents is pretty straightforward: it amounts to dragging or trailing a lure behind a boat. If you are trolling alone, you simply sit in the stern with one hand on the outboard's control handle and the other on the rod. You can use the same lures you normally fish on rivers.

Simple up-river harling: one hand on the outboard control, the other on the rod.

You can troll both up against the current and down with it.

The biggest challenge to upriver trolling is learning to control the speed and depth of your lure, since it will be working more or less continuously against a current. Remember we want lure speeds of around 2ft/s (*c.* 1½mph or 0.5m/s) for cold water and 5ft/s (*c.* 3½mph or 1m/s) for warm.

So how do you know how fast the lure is travelling? It turns out that our desired speed range is roughly the difference between a leisure walking pace and a brisk walking pace. So what I do is tramp along the bank for a few yards (metres) before getting in the boat to get a rough idea of the current's strength and speed. Once on the water I can make adjustments with the throttle to keep the right speed. Remember, it's the

lure's water speed, not land speed you need to control.

Down-current trolling is a bit trickier but it's often more effective, like upstreaming a lure from the bank when the water is more or less clear and warmer. Getting the right speed here means watching the current and not the bank. You want to be moving a little faster than the water's speed: just fast enough to keep your lure moving as it should. Spoons and spinners work well here because both maintain their action when working with the current.

How about controlling depth? Some anglers like to get a lure down by letting out a very long line (*see* Still-Water Trolling below). Others, myself included, opt for adding a dropper-weight (*see* Ledger Rigs below) to a shorter line of 30–50yd (30–50m). This way I can keep in direct touch with the bottom via the dropper-weight, so that I can adjust to changes in depth and current by changing my boat's speed.

Usually I fish only one rod. On some waters that's all you are allowed, but if you can, fishing two rods doubles your chances of a take, if not a netted fish. The problem with fishing two rods is that one rod fishes unattended. I usually rest that one in front of the oar lock angled out over the side. Some anglers wedge it under the seat.

When a fish hits the free rod, you won't be able to react as quickly as you normally would. So, ideally you want the fish to hook itself and to stay hooked at least long enough for you to grab the rod and take control. You can do a couple of things to increase your chances here. One is to make sure the unattended set-up is loaded with monofilament line. Mono has more stretch than braid, so it's harder for a fish to slacken it once hooked. Normally the forward momentum of the boat alone will keep sufficient tension on the line until you can take over (*see* Playing Fish in Currents below). You can also increase your hold rate by using either the very best super-sharp cone-tip trebles you can find, or round-bend Siwash single hooks (*see* About Hooks in Chapter 2). For the other rod – the one you are holding – you can use the same set up as when working from the bank.

LURES AND RIGS

As I mentioned in Chapter 2, you can troll any lure either flat-line (unweighted) or on a ledger rig (*see* Ledger Rigs below). You'll need to experiment to see which lures keep the best action at different trolling speeds. Because you

Harling up a gentle glide by oar-power.

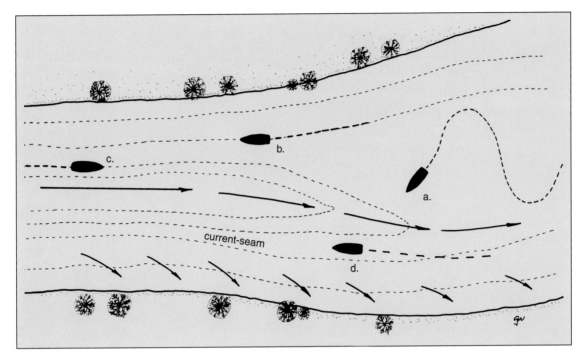

Harling patterns: 'S' pattern (a); trolling a contour up-current (b); trolling a contour down-current (c); trolling a seam up-current (d).

are working against the current, actual water speed of your lure is often faster than when trolling in still water – commonly up around 3½mph (1.6m/s). This is too fast for many spoons but jigging spoons, crankbaits like Rapalas, long-bladed spinners like Mepps Aglia Long all work well at these higher speeds.

If you are fishing flat-line, without additional weights, you should be able to keep track of a spoon's or plug's action either by feeling it or, if it's on the unmanned rod, by seeing the rod tip pulsating. If you can't, you'll need to pull it in to check for tangles or debris. It's impossible to detect a spinner's action when trolling it off a ledger rig, so you'll need to check it more frequently for foul-ups.

S-PATTERN TROLLING

The recommended manoeuvre when trolling up or down-current is to work your boat in 'S' curves. Under most situations this is clearly the best way to cover the water. It also makes the trailing lure a little more attractive than on a straight pull, since it imparts some irregularity in its path, depth and speed.

However, there are times when the 'S' manoeuvre isn't your best move. This is when you are harling a river with a deep 'canyon' or 'bathtub' profile and you want to keep the lure running right along the bottom. Working the boat in 'S' curves under these conditions, it's nearly impossible to keep the lure running at the right depth without constantly lengthening and shortening the line as the boat moves from shallow edge to deeper mid-stream water and back again. This isn't a big issue when you are trailing a lure high in the water under warmer conditions, but it is when the target water is no more than a foot (30cm) or so off bottom.

Trolling up a current seam.

CONTOUR TROLLING

On my local river we've devised an alternative manoeuvre for bottom-trolling. You could call it 'contour trolling'. This is done by first setting the depth of your lure by letting out line until the ledger weight hits bottom. Once the lure is where it should be depth-wise, you want to try to keep it there along the whole route by choosing a path that covers water of about the same depth, all the way up or down the piece of river you want to fish. This usually means you end up running your boat up or down the river in a route that is more or less parallel to the shore. It also means you won't be covering any stretch of river in one pass like you would if you were following an 'S' path. Instead, you cover it by going up- or down-river several times, each time picking a path that runs along a different bottom contour.

You can tell if you are following the contour and your lure is fishing along it, if the dropper-weight taps bottom every now and then. I like to feel it hit about every fifteen or twenty seconds. When it doesn't, I adjust the boat's direction until it does.

TROLLING SEAMS

Another way to cover the water when trolling is to target only the current seams. This can be especially effective when fish are running up-river but it takes a lot of experience and an intimate knowledge of the currents.

Running fish usually take the easiest route by finding seams along current edges. 'Seam trolling' calls for essentially shadowing these routes. To make it more challenging, seams change location with water level and current strength – typically closer to shore in heavy water and further out in lower water. Learning to troll the seams takes experience, but it's hard to beat for efficiency.

Back-trolling

Downriver-drifting or back-trolling is probably the single most effective way to cover a stretch of river. It amounts to backing your boat down river in a zigzag pattern – just a little slower than the current – while keeping your lure drifting deeply on about 100ft (30m) of line. As when drifting from the bank, it's imperative that you keep your lure bouncing along the bottom, and this is easier to do with the more sensitive and responsive braid line. You will still get plenty of

hang-ups when back-trolling but it's much easier to free snags from a boat.

Traditional back-trolling calls for an angler and an oarsman. When I'm taking an angler out, I man the oars and we drift down without power. The routine is to first motor up to the head of the water we want to cover, usually trolling a spoon or plug along the way. Once at the top, we cut the motor and start our drift. I keep the bow nosed up-current and break our speed by dragging the oars. I also angle the prow a little one way or the other, so that the boat 'slides' diagonally from bank to bank. The angler sits in the bow, or middle, facing down-current while working the lure along the bottom just like drifting from the bank.

Now that's the ideal situation: one oarsman, one angler. But when I'm in the boat alone I have to make a few adjustments. I troll

Back-trolling with oarsman and angler.

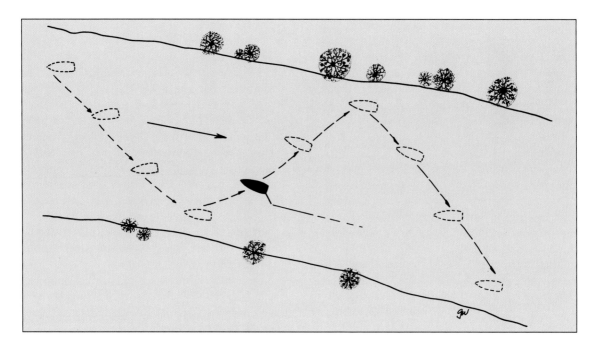

ABOVE: Back-trolling.

LEFT: Back-trolling alone by using the outboard to control drift speed and course.

upstream as before but when I drift down, I use the motor to control the drift. I sit in the stern with one hand on the outboard control, the other on the rod. I position myself so I'm facing sideways toward the bank. This way I can keep a better sense of drift speed and also my boat's course. It's pretty easy to weave the boat from bank to bank in a gentle down-current zigzag using the motor's rudder. It is harder to keep your lure bouncing ideally along the bottom with one hand while controlling the drift of the boat with the other. It's a matter of co-ordination but you can get surprisingly good at it with practice.

Unlike trolling up-current, I use one rod when drifting downstream. It's hard enough to pull off a good drift with one set up, impossible with two. Drift spoons are my first choice for back-trolling but for very rocky or snaggy

Drift-ice requires some adjustments to your presentation.

bottoms, many use more buoyant lures like diving plugs or Devons run off ledger rigs.

As in drifting from the bank, you can also jig the lure down in bigger steps – this is drift jigging from a boat.

The only real drawback to harling is that it takes up a lot of space on the river. Your slowly zigzagging boat and line can easily interfere with anglers working from the bank. Code of the river: bank fisherman have the right of way.

A word to the wise: in tough conditions keep it simple. When I'm harling alone in heavy water or in a stiff wind, I fish one rod and I keep my tackle set-up simple. Playing and landing a fish with one hand while manoeuvring the boat with the other is challenging enough in easy water, it's much harder in a strong current or when

the wind is fighting you. Even a tangled line becomes a big problem. So I save the second rod for easier conditions.

Tip: Drifting Down-Current First

On larger rivers it's common to troll up-current first, then to drift slowly down-current over the same water. But on small rivers or streams, and especially if the water is clear, it's best to begin from up above the target water and drift down into it so your lure covers the fish before your line and boat.

Dealing with Drift-Ice

There are few situations that make currents nearly un-fishable. One is drifting ice. This is a common problem on many rivers and tailwaters during early winter before the water has frozen solid or in early spring before it's completely melted. Faced with a dense flow of free-floating ice-sheets ranging from pizza to table-top size, many anglers simply go home until conditions improve. But for the die-hards (some would say pig-headed) there are a couple of things you can try before packing up.

If you are working from the shore, the first thing to do is look for any pockets of ice-free water. You can sometimes find small openings just below points, islets, outcroppings, piers, bridges and similar structures that divert ice-flow. If so, fish these as you normally would. If not, then you've got essentially two options: (1) deep-drifting with the flow, and (2) deep-sweeping under it. Before you try either you might want to consider changing to a heavy monofilament line of say 20 to 30lb test, if you aren't already using one. Mono is much more resistant to abrasion from flowing ice than braid, although not as easy to control through a drift. It's a trade-off.

Drifting with the Ice
The key to pulling off a good deep drift in currents carrying lots of loose ice is to get your lure down very quickly and to keep it drifting at the same speed as the flowing ice. For this I use a heavier drift spoon than I normally would for the same currents, something in the $1\frac{1}{4}$–$1\frac{3}{8}$oz (35–40g) range. Don't worry if that seems

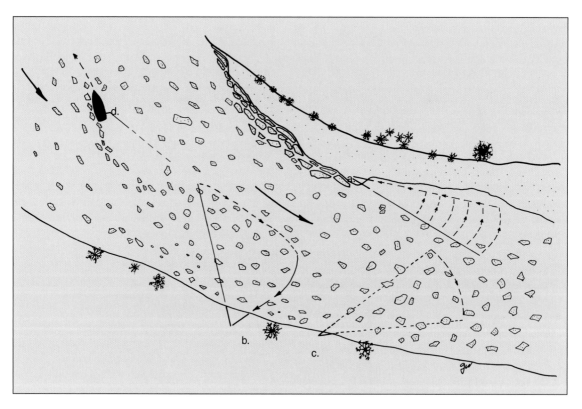

Dealing with drift-ice: fishing ice-free pockets (a); drifting with the ice (b); sweeping under the ice (c); harling against drift-ice (d).

excessive, for ice-water sea trout bigger is often better anyway. Otherwise carry out the drift in pretty much the same way as you would in ice-free flows. You might have to manoeuvre your spoon a bit to get it down through the surface ice if it's a dense flow. It's common to land your spoon on top of an ice sheet. Don't worry. Just slid it off and get it down to the bottom as quickly as you can.

Unlike normal drifting it's important to keep your rod tip up, as high as you can through the drift. That way you keep as much line out of the water as possible and minimize chances that the surface ice grabs it too soon and pulls the spoon back up to the surface. This means you'll need to give line freely as the spoon drifts along, either by opening the bale arm (normally to be avoided) or releasing the reverse brake and letting the spoon's momentum take line as needed.

Unlike drifting in ice-free currents, you won't be able to fish the spoon around at the end of the drift. Inevitably, once the spoon is below you, the surface ice will grab the line and quickly 'pulley' the spoon up to the surface. (This is where the more abrasion-resistant mono comes in.) Even so, it's pretty common that your spoon ends up hooking the edge of a drifting ice sheet and you find yourself battling it as it moves downstream until either the spoon breaks free or you run out of line. Personally, I try to avoid the whole end-scenario by pulling my spoon up and out of the flow and back home before it starts to make the turn at the bottom of the drift. It works about half of the time.

Sweeping Under the Ice

You can also try sweeping a lure under the ice, provided the flow isn't too dense. The key here is to wait for an opening in the flow wide enough to get the lure and entire line under the surface. For this operation, heavy monofilament line, which sinks, is a must. (If I had to deal with these conditions more than I do I'd consider experimenting with steel or lead-core line.)

For under-ice sweeping I use the same swimming or jigging spoon I normally would. You can't be too picky when choosing an opening to cast to. Take any opening from an upstream to a downstream angle. The point is to get the whole set-up from lure to rod tip down below the level of the ice. Once you find a window, make the cast and, as soon as the lure hits the water, plunge the rod tip down as deeply as you can. You will probably need to reel in a little line to keep a belly from forming in the middle. Once the lure and line are 'safely' under the ice, you can simply let the current sweep it around as in a normal deep-drift. You can't mend line of course, but you can give out line to keep the lure running deep and to extend the sweep as long as possible. If you are lucky you can fish the lure all the way around the turn at the bottom and get it back home without coming in contact with the flowing surface ice. Good luck.

Harling Against the Ice

If you have a harling boat you're in a much better position to deal with drift-ice. The tactic is to troll upstream so you can use the boat to 'run interference' by clearing a short path of water for your lure and line to run through. You can use the same basic ledger set-up you would in ice-free cold-water conditions (see Ledger Rigs below), only it's a good idea to use a thicker than normal monofilament mainline and a heavier dropper-weight. (You can always use a thinner leader if water clarity seems to call for it.) The thicker mainline will resist ice-abrasion and the heavier dropper-weight will allow you to troll a shorter line than normal – about 20yd (20m) is typical – so you can keep your tackle fishing in the ice-free window your boat has cleared. Don't worry about spooking these slow-metabolism ice-water trout unless you are working over very clear or shallow water.

If you can keep good contact with the bottom, then trolling in a diagonal or zigzag pattern is ideal because it tends to clear a wider path in the on-coming ice. If contour trolling is called for you'll want to position your rod straight out the back of the boat because your ice-free path won't be as wide.

Fishing Currents Through the Ice

Where I fish, the rivers freeze over from about December to April. That means, to get to over-wintering sea trout you've got two options: find short stretches of open tailwater below dams or drill your own holes through the ice. For tailwaters, standard river presentations work. For fishing through the ice, you'll need more specialized methods and tackle. But forget about tip-ups and those little pimpling rod-reel outfits you use for perch and char. Taking sea trout through the ice is a lot closer to harling in terms of tactics – only the water is harder!

I used to think ice-fishing was a last resort when you couldn't find open water. Boy was I wrong! Apart from keeping you fishing all winter, ice-fishing lets you cover and take ice-water sea trout effectively (*see* Winter River Tactics in Chapter 4). You can literally dangle a very slow-moving lure right in front of their nose and keep it there long enough to get a strike. On my river, experienced icers clean up on a good day, but success has its cost. You've got to be willing to spend cold hours on the ice, and you've got to be willing to drill a lot of holes.

Here's the routine. First, you want a stretch of good holding water. Most icers target places they already know will be holding over-wintering fish (*see* Winter River Tactics in Chapter 4). If you aren't certain, you can work to a grid, just like you do when casting on foot.

Your first move is to drill a series of holes in a line perpendicular to the bank across the whole

A lone icer works a set of holes on a lower stretch of frozen river.

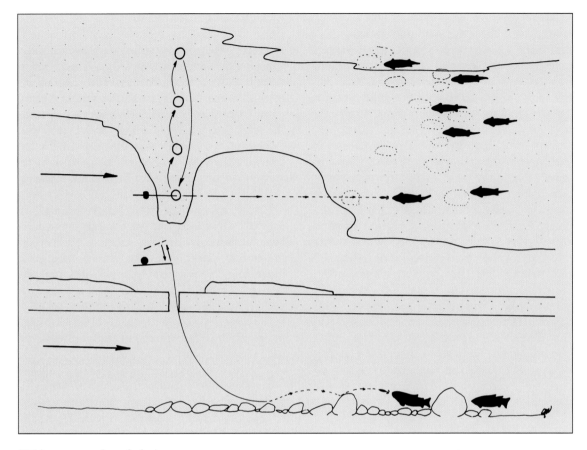

Fishing currents through the ice.

piece of target water. How many holes depends on how wide the holding water is and how much you want to work. Usually not bank-to-bank because the still-water edges generally hold fewer fish and there isn't enough current to work the lures properly. Obviously you can't sweep or drift lures when fishing through a hole. You're limited to covering fish more or less lying directly down-current by backing-down your lure, hanging it or jigging it. This means you can space the holes right down to a few feet (1m) – the size of the strike zone – if you've got the energy.

Most icers drill holes with hand augers. Some use gas-powered models. If you don't mind the noise and don't need the exercise, power augers can rip through a couple of feet (60cm) of ice in

a matter of seconds. But the standard 4¼in (11cm) drill bit is too small. You want one with at least a 6in (15.5cm) diameter; 8in (20.5cm) if you are expecting fish over 10lb (4kg). Some say it's a good idea to drill holes the day before to give fish a chance to settle, especially when using power bores. The only drawback is you'll probably have to clear each hole of thin ice before you start fishing. Once the holes are in, the tactic is to work across the transect. The typical method is to fish a lure down-current, anywhere from 30 to 50yd (30–50m); to hang it for a few seconds to a few minutes at the end, then to jig it back up until it's home. Some do this once before moving to the next hole, others stay with a hole longer.

After working over a series of holes it's common to repeat the operation, starting at the first hole. Or you can start a new series of holes, either up- or down-river from the original transect. Just like when casting to a grid, new transects are spaced so your presentations overlap – that's usually anywhere from 30 to 50yd (30–50m).

Icers in my area use the very same lures we use for casting to ice-water sea trout. These are mainly big shiny or strong-pattern swimming and jigging spoons. (Ledgered flutter-spoons would probably work well too.) They also use pretty much the same tackle, but most find it's easier to work lures through ice with a shorter rod. Companies like Normark and Abu make rods just for this. They are about 2½–4ft (0.8–1.2m) long and strong enough to hold a big sea trout. Some companies also make mono designed for ice-fishing, like Normark Arctic. But most icers I know use standard high-quality monofilament. The only other special equipment you need, besides really warm clothes and good boots, is a plastic ladle to clear new ice that builds up in the holes.

Tip: Deeper, Slower, Bigger and Later for the Lunkers

If you are after big fish there are a few things you can do to up your chances. First, because bigger, stronger fish tend to hold in the security of deeper, heavier currents (because they can), then target these. Second, make your offering worth a lunker's trouble. Big fish are more cost-conscious than smaller fish. A bigger lure fished slower will move them more easily than a smaller one fished fast. Third, concentrate your efforts after hours, from dusk till dawn. That's when bigger feeding fish hunt most actively and even big spawners are more willing to hit a lure.

Still-Water Presentations

Pursuing sea trout in still waters presents the spin-angler with some new challenges. First, there is a lot more water to deal with. Somebody once said that 90 per cent of the fish hold in 10 per cent of the water. Fine. Which 10 per cent? We can use what we know about sea-trout behaviour to narrow this down to the most likely holding water. But when faced with an entire lake or estuary, not to mention the sea, that's still a lot of water.

Knowledge of sea-trout behaviour and an intimate familiarity with the water in question have traditionally divided successful still-water sea-trouters from the rest. Today, more and more anglers are tipping the scales in their favour by employing advanced sonar and navigational technologies (*see* Fish Finders and GPS below). Regardless, the basic approach is covering as much target water as possible, whether on foot or with a boat.

The second challenge to still-water fishing is controlling lure speed and depth. In rivers it's basically a matter of working your lure with or against the current, near the bottom or near the surface. To be successful in still waters, you've got to learn ways to control your lure's speed and movements without the help of the current. You also need to find ways to keep it fishing at just the right depth, even in very deep water. So, still-water presentations also emphasize lure control.

The third challenge is edgy fish. Still water is often clearer than flowing water. Sea trout can see farther so they feel less secure. Successful still-water presentations also need to incorporate stealth.

Fan Casting or Round-the-Clock

This is the standard way of presenting a lure on foot or from a drifting boat. Basically, the targeted water (or fish) is chosen and a series of casts are made in a fan pattern to cover it.

On Foot
The most efficient tact when working from the

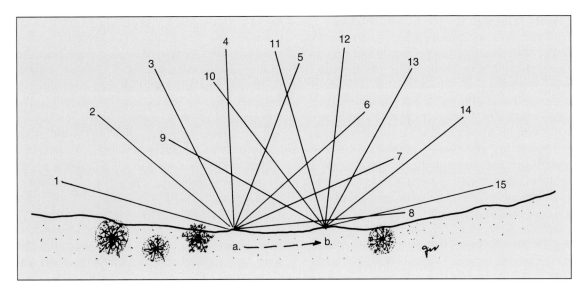

Fan or round-the-clock casting.

shore is to position yourself on a small promontory or to wade out so you can make casts around the entire radius from bank to bank. It's a good idea to cover the near-shore water first by making a few cast from well back. Move cautiously and keep low if visibility is high. Space casts as you would in a current. You can go a little wider than on the river – up to 6ft (2m) if the water is clear.

Just as in currents, a high, fast, steady retrieve works best when the water is warmer (above 56°F or 13°C), while a slow, deep, retrieve is your best bet if it's cold, say under 47°F (8°C). But when the water is in the ideal range (47–56°F or 4–8°C), try to vary the lure's course and speed as much as possible. The sink-and-draw retrieve is a standard (*see* Drift-Jigging above). Or you can alternate with a flat zigzag retrieve by moving the rod tip abruptly from side to side while reeling in.

Since the ability to cast a very long line allows you to cover more water quickly, many shore anglers opt for longer rods of up to 10ft (3m), and thinner lines of around 10lb test for the extra distance. Swimming spoons, conventional spinners and coast wobblers are popular choices for still-water casting. Many anglers move along the shore while making long, perpendicular casts every few paces or so. A better move is to overlap fan patterns. This way potential takers are covered from several directions.

From a Boat
Casting from an anchored or drifting boat is an even more effective way of working still water. As when harling, a boat lets you position yourself more ideally for covering targeted water and you can cover more of it from each position. You can fan-cast literally the full way round-the-clock. A boat also allows you to cover the shallows without spooking feeding fish by making a long cast from further out. You can also follow schools of feeding fish as they move along the shore or up and down an estuary. Hugh Falkus reported success at night by casting a surface plug at right angles to the path of a rowed boat and allowing it to swing round behind.

Don't forget stealth, especially in clear, shallow and smooth unbroken water. Cut the motor as soon as possible. Mind splashing oars, and the boat's moving shadow. Keep low and quiet inside the boat.

Fishing Through the Ice in Still Waters

Ice-fishing for sea trout in still waters is carried out in the same way as it is on frozen rivers. Only it's a lot more challenging.[46] In the much vaster expanse of a frozen lake or estuary, where to place your holes is the million-dollar-question. Those that are consistently successful have intimate knowledge of the water and know the places sea trout are most likely to be over-wintering, like around feeder streams and underwater springs.

Hole placement is the key to scoring through the ice in still water

Unlike river tactics, holes aren't drilled in tightly spaced transects, but in more irregular patterns spaced from 5–15ft (1.5–4.5m) apart. The tactic is to cover targeted areas, quickly searching for fish. Typically the angler spends no more than a few minutes at any hole before moving to the next. If no takers are found, a new set of holes is drilled and sampled in turn. Only after a taking fish is located does the icer settle into fishing the location more thoroughly. Since sea trout often travel in small groups, it's not uncommon for the same hole or adjacent holes to produce several fish.

Lure presentation is also a little different than on rivers. Without a current to carry lures downstream to waiting fish, the still water icer is limited to working water directly below the hole. Jigging light-weight spoons is one method but jigs designed to swim in erratic circles seem to be more effective (*see* Jigging Spoons in Chapter 2). As for ice drills, rods and

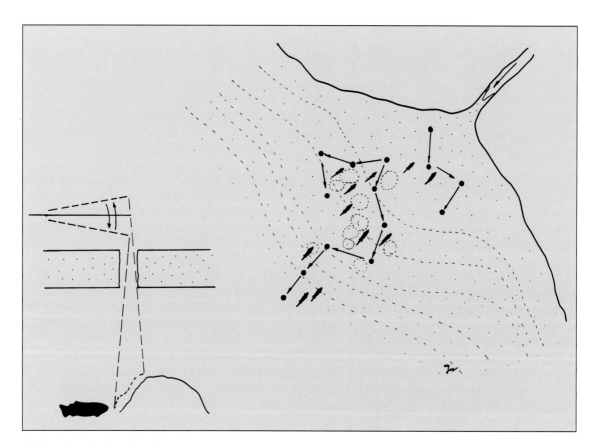

Fishing through the ice in still water.

A light-trolling set-up: simple and effective.

reels, the same used for ice-fishing in currents will do (*see* Fishing Currents Through the Ice above)

Light Trolling

Because coverage usually translates to success on still waters, it's hard to beat trolling in terms of hooked-fish per day. It's simply much easier to cover more water more thoroughly and in less time than on foot. You can also target pieces of water completely out of casting reach.

If you are content to pursue sea trout in the top 15–20ft (4.5–6m) of water, where sea trout usually are, then you can master this method using pretty much the same techniques and equipment you do when harling on the river. Once you've narrowed down the water to likely holding zones, it's a matter of covering them

by trailing one or more lures, either flatline (unweighted) or ledger-rigged, behind a small boat.

Trolling Speed

Determining lure speed and depth are the biggest challenges. This can be a lot trickier on open, still water, where you can't always count on a shallow bottom or nearby shoreline features as reference points. Most anglers figure this out through trial and error, but there are some rough guidelines to go by.

I already mentioned that speeds between 1½ and 3½mph (0.5–1.6m/s) or about the difference between a leisure and a brisk walking pace, seem to be the most effective for sea trout, depending on water and light conditions. So, if you can see the bank, you can probably get your

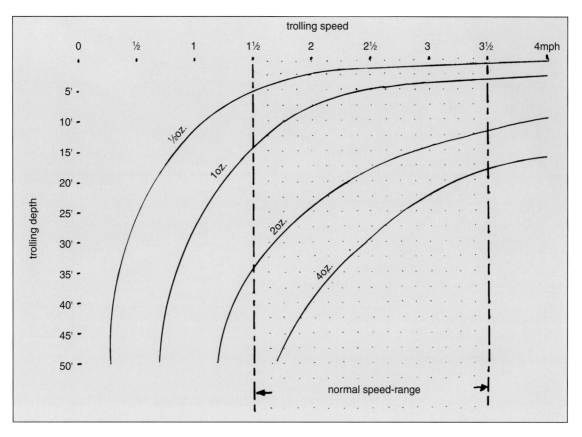

Trolling depths for 100ft (30m) of 20lb test monofilament line or 50lb test braid at different trolling speeds and lure (or lure plus sinker) weights based on Ray Rychnovsky's published graphs.

boat moving roughly at those rates. With time you will also get a feel for the right speed by watching the action of your favourite lures.

The alternative is to get a speed indicator. For most harling or light-trolling boats, full GPS navigational systems are an overkill. But Luhr-Jensen makes a manual model called Luhr-Speed Trolling Speed Indicator that fits the bill. It mounts on the side or stern and measures even slow-trolling speeds pretty accurately.

Trolling Depth
How deep your lure fishes will depend mainly on its weight, your boat's speed and, to a lesser degree, how thick the line is. One trolling expert, Ray Rychnovsky, has published a series

of useful graphs on this.[47] For example, a 1oz-spoon trolled on 30yd of 20lb (9kg) test mono at a speed of about 1½mph (0.5m/s) – typical cold-water speed – fishes at a depth of about 15ft (4.5m). But at higher speeds of around 3½mph (1.6m/s) – typical warm-water trolling speed – the same lure fishes much higher up, in the top 5ft (1.5m) of water. Some old-school loch trollers, like Hamish Young, get a little more depth by letting out longer lines, up to 100yd (100m),[48] but it's more common to simply add weight via a ledger rig. To increase vertical coverage, many trollers fish up to three rods, each trailing its lure at a different distance behind, usually between 30 and 50yd (30–50m).

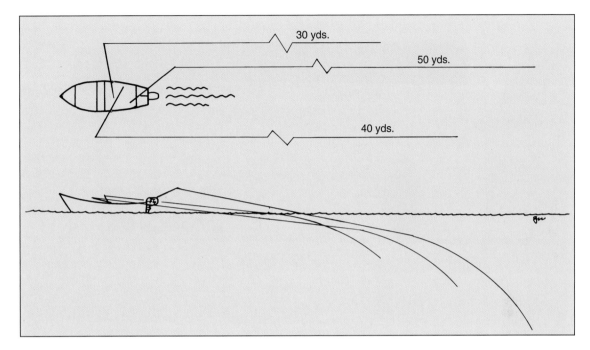

Positioning three trolling rods.

Trolling Coverage

The best way to work the target water is in an 'S' pattern. This causes the lure to fish at irregular speeds and depths. On the inside swing of the boat, the lure drops deeper and slows down; on the outside turn, it speeds up and rises – movements much more attractive to sea trout than anything straight and regular. Some trollers add further variation by giving the rod a sharp jerk from time to time, or by rapidly alternating the boat's speed between fast and slow over short distances, or by bringing the boat to full stop then restarting again.

Trolling Lures

You can troll almost any lure. The trick is to find one that keeps its action at the desired speed. The standard Toby casting spoon in $\frac{1}{3}$–1oz (10–28g) weights has probably taken more sea trout on trolling rigs than any other lure. Flutter-spoons also work well at lower trolling speeds, and Rapala-like plugs are a good choice for higher speeds. Whatever you are trolling, remember to control for line twist with a good ball-bearing swivel set-up.

Outboards versus Oars

Most anglers use a small 4–10hp outboard to maintain trolling speeds, either gas-fuelled or electric, but there is nothing to say you can't use the oars. Many experienced loch trollers prefer rowing because it's easier to keep low speeds, and it's quieter and less prone to spook fish in the shallows. Many even pad the oarlocks with leather to cut down noise. So if you are up to it, try cutting the motor once you've reached your target water and trolling manually. At the very least you'll get some exercise and save some gas!

Otter Boards and Planer Boards

Old timers in my region sometimes troll with a home-made contraption called an otter board or otter door. It's basically a frame of wood with

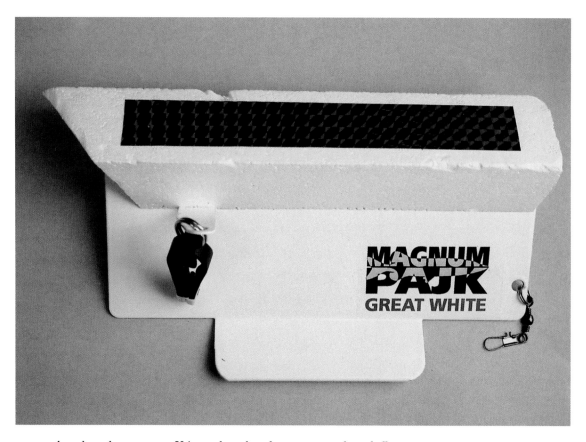

ABOVE: A modern planer. BELOW: Using a planer board to cover near-shore shallows.

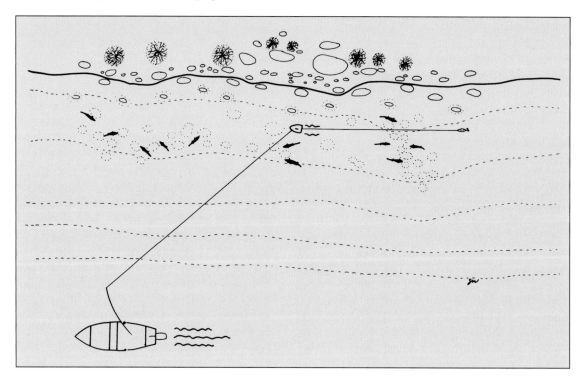

a movable keel that you drag behind your boat on the end of a thin rope. It's put together in a clever way so that it sweeps from side to side in a wide arc behind the boat like a little water skier. You attach your fishing line to this thing by a quick-release trigger. When it all works the way it should, it lets your boat slowly forward while your lure is being fished in a nice effective 'S' pattern behind. Once a fish takes, the line releases and you play the fish freely.

However, otter boards are cumbersome and prone to tangling at the wrong times, so few anglers use them any more. Modern versions, called planer boards, are a little easier to use but still require careful management to avoid cock-ups. Modern versions like the popular Yellow Bird Surface Planer or the Magnum Pajk Big White don't sweep back and forth but keep a pre-set course to one side. Their greatest value is for covering shallow near-shore water without having to run the boat through it first and risk spooking fish. It has become a favourite technique for taking spring sea trout in some Swedish estuaries.

Deep Trolling
We know that sea trout stay in the top 15–20ft (4.5–6m) of water most of the time. We also know that sometimes they go deeper. Usually this is to escape uncomfortably warm summer water or when they are following schools of herring or sprat off-shore 50–60ft (15.5–18.5m) down (*see* Chapter 4). This is nothing compared to deep-water fish like lake trout (char) or even brownies that routinely hunt at depths beyond 100ft (30m), but it's still too deep for conventional light-trolling gear. Sure, you can add more and more weight to a standard ledger rig. Slowly trolling a 2oz lure-and-sinker set-up will get you down to about 35ft (11m), adding another ounce will get you down past 40ft (12m), but most anglers find the extra weight puts too much strain on their tackle. It's also more cumbersome and definitely less pleasurable to play a fish with several ounces of lead along for the ride. If you want to cover deeper sea trout effectively, you're much better off

biting-the-bullet and putting together a deep-trolling outfit.

Until pretty recently, most sea trout were taken by anglers deep-trolling for salmon off-shore or in deep lakes like Loch Lomond in Scotland. Now more trollers are setting up to target sea trout at depths up to about 60ft (18.5m). Deep trolling has become especially popular off the Jutland coast, where it accounts for most of the really big sea trout taken each year in Denmark. Because of the tackle requirements, deep trolling has become pretty specialized. I'm only going to touch on a few basics. If you really want to get into it, there are plenty of good guide-books you can turn to, starting with *The Troller's Handbook* by Ray Rychnovsky.

Downriggers
Deep trolling all started with the invention of the downrigger. In his classic manual *Sea Trout Fishing* Hugh Falkus described an early home-made rig for fishing a light bait off a small dinghy at a controlled depth without any added weight on the line. Modern versions work the same. They are essentially small winches you attach to the boat's gunnels loaded with 50–200ft (15.5–60m) of stainless steel wire attached to a heavy weight or cannonball (normally around 10lb or 4.5kg).

To get your lure down with a downrigger, you let out 10–20ft (3–6m) of line behind the boat. Then you connect the line to the downrigger cable by a little pinch pad release, which looks like a clothes pin. Once connected, you lower the cannonball into the water to your desired trolling depth by reading the counter either on the winch or the reel. When a fish hits the lure the release pops open, leaving you to play the fish on a free unweighted line. Cannon makes the most popular models.

Diving Planes
These work just like they sound. They take your line and lure to deep water by planing down through it. You attach the diver to your line about 4–6ft (1–2m) ahead of the lure. Different models run at different depths, anywhere from

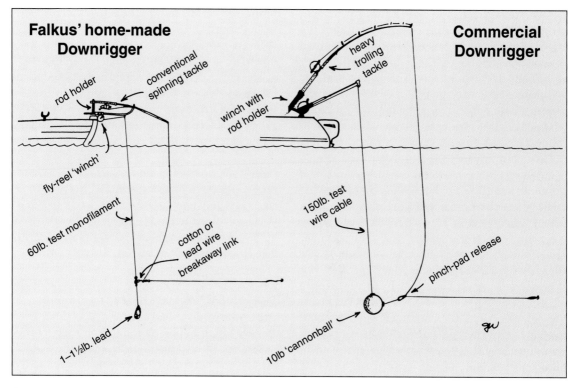

Downriggers, old and new.

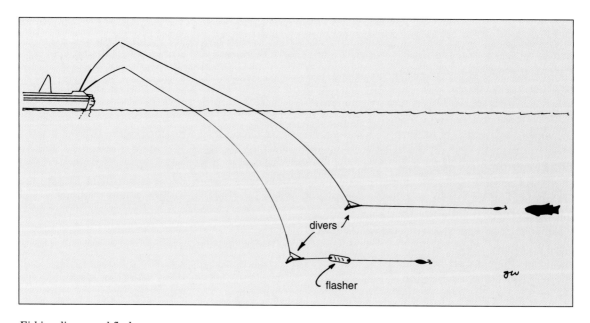

Fishing divers sand flasher.

10 to 75ft (3–23m). One drawback is that, unlike a downrigger, a diver stays on the line. They are designed so the planer part can be tripped (usually by jerking on the line) so it rides on the line with less resistance while you are playing the fish. Even so, planers can add anywhere from 1 to 3oz (30–90g) extra weight, so they are used with heavier lines, usually 0.02–0.03in (0.50–0.70mm) mono.

One great advantage of diving planes is they can be adjusted so they run out to either side of the boat. This means you can fish them in combination with downriggers or flat-lines fished off the stern. The most popular diver models are Luhr-Jensen's Pink Lady and Dipsy Diver, U-Charter's Slide Diver, Blue Fox's Wiggler and Normark's Trophy.

Flashers and Dodgers
These are often added to downrigger set-ups. Both are basically very large rectangular steel or plastic slab-spoons without the hooks. Most have shiny prism finishes that attract fish to the lure by simulating the kind of reflection given off by a school of bait fish. They also impart additional action to the trailing lure. Dodgers like Jensen, Sep's, Les Davis, Gold Star and Red Eye wobble and roll. Flashers like Alaskan Eagle, Abe'n Al, Hot Spot and Silver Horde have a more deliberate roll-with-tail-snap action. Just like spoons, different dodgers and flashers have different speed tolerances.

Rods, Reels and Lines
If you are only fishing off a downrigger, you can use the same tackle you do for harling and light trolling. If you fish with diving planes, flashers or dodgers you will need a heavier outfit to cope with extra drag and heavier line. Shimano Catana Downrigger, Beastmaster Downrigger and XFX AX Downrigger rods teamed with Shimano Tekota, Charter Special and TR reels loaded with 600–1,000ft (185–300m) of 20–40lb test line are popular set-ups. Some anglers prefer the much thinner braids to mono, in order to minimize the drag from the heavier test lines.

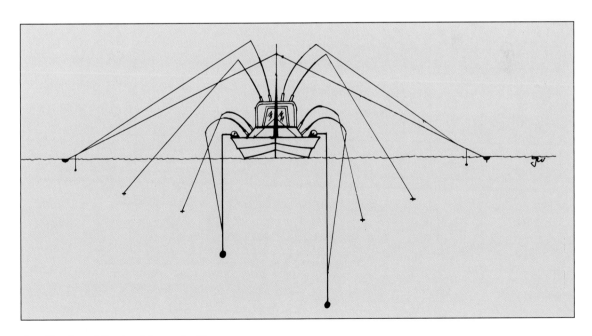

A trolling boat fully rigged for competition.

Depending on regulations, deep trollers usually fish more rods than light trollers. Tournament boats routinely fish six to ten lures simultaneously off divers, planers and downriggers by positioning as many rods around the boat.

Fish Finders and GPS
Sonar fish finders have taken much of the guesswork out of working large, open waters and most deep trollers are outfitted with one. They can't tell you whether the fish you see on the monitor are sea trout or, say, salmon or pike, but they can tell you about how big and how many they are and at what depth they are holding. Even if you don't see big fish on the screen, it can help you locate likely target water by reading water temperatures, depth and bottom contours, even bottom composition (soft or hard) and by locating underwater structures and even shoals of bait fish.

Most fish finders are designed to work best at depths below 10ft (3m) but side-scanning models for shallow water trolling and harling are also available. There are even smaller portable units made for ice-fishing or working from the bank, but as far as I know these haven't (yet) won a place among sea-trouters. Nowadays there are models to fit almost any budget. Those made by Lawrance and Computrol (Fishing Buddy) are the most popular.

GPS (Global Positioning System) is a navigational device that pinpoints your boat's position and monitors its speed. Because it helps in navigating in fog or limited visibility it has become an essential safety feature on boats trolling offshore. It also allows you to record the location of hot spots so you can return to them later. Lawrance makes these too.

Boats
Some anglers run simple downrigger and diver

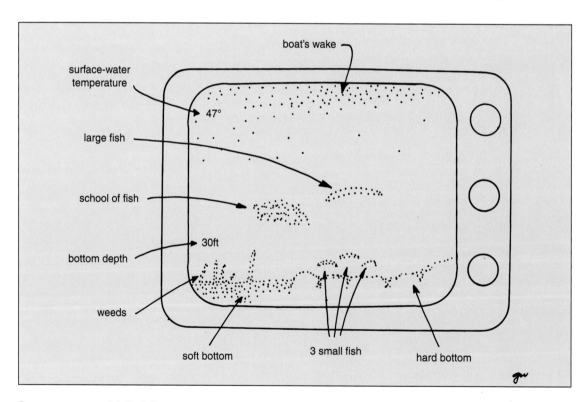

Images on a sonar fish finder's screen.

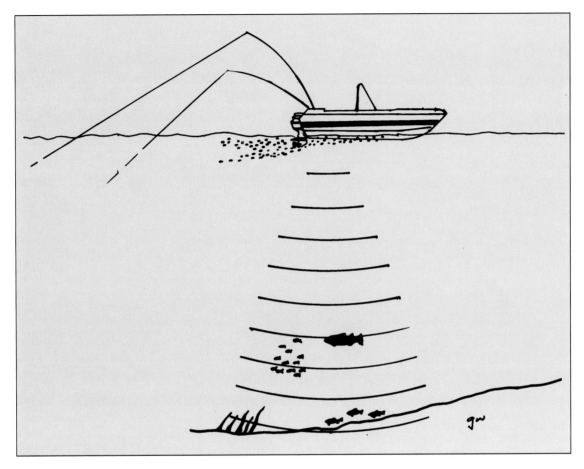

Sonar coverage under the boat.

set-ups off the same boats they use for harling or light trolling. That's OK on some waters but if you want to head out into bigger and potentially rougher open waters fitted out with a lot of special trolling gear, you'll need a bigger, safer boat. A fairly typical model for deep trolling would run 15–20ft (4.5–6m) in length, have suitably deep draft for rough conditions, an enclosed or partly enclosed cabin, console steering and a 10–50hp outboard. To save time and fuel, many trollers opt for a two-motor montage: a big cruising motor with maybe 100–175hp to get you to and from the target water and a smaller one of 10–25hp for trolling.

Deep-Trolling Lures

Any lure can be deep trolled. Among tournament anglers, trolling spoons (flutter-spoons) are the most popular. Ismo King, Ismo Quack, Ismo Magnum, Pirate, Northern King Magnum, Iron Horn, Break Point and Big Horn probably lead the pack of favourites. Plugs like Apex, Rapala and Abu are also effective.

Playing and Landing Sea Trout

Most sea-trouters have their own opinion on the best way to deal with a fish once it's on the line.

Keeping pressure on a hooked fish is the key to landing it.

My own approach to playing a sea trout is pretty straightforward. I start out with two assumptions. The first is that your line and connections are up to the job. The second is that you've got a reel with a good drag system and that it's set correctly.

I usually fish a main line with 20lb (9kg) break strength and a leader of 18lb (8kg) strength. I set my drag to a little below that of the leader's break point. Normally, I do this by feel since I know my gear pretty well. But if it's a new reel or a different strength line, I set the drag first time with the help of my fish scale. I tie the leader to the hook on the scale, close the drag and pull the line until it breaks. I read the scale. Then I adjust the drag until it lets out line at about 80 per cent of the reading. This is also a

good exercise because it lets you see how strong your knots are. You'll learn that it's usually at these joints that the line gives, and at lower pressure than the published strength for that line! On my reel the drag has a lever with three settings: normal, looser and tighter. I make my initial setting at 'normal'. That way I can quickly loosen or tighten it if I need to when I'm playing a fish.

Assuming good lines and connections and a well-set drag, there is no reason any sea trout should ever break you off. Given that, the trick to successfully playing a fish is keeping continuous pressure on it from the moment you've set the hook until you've landed it. It's during a momentary slackening of the line that most fish throw the hook.

What is continuous pressure? It means keeping a good bend in the rod. That's easier said than done, but here is where mono has clear advantages over braids. Because mono is more elastic, it's easier to keep pressure on a fish – even when it's charging toward you – than it is with low or non-stretch braids.

Playing Fish in Currents

Let's take a typical hook-up on the river. First you feel the fish strike and you set the hook. Your rod is already bowed back with the handle pointing nearly straight up and the tip arched over. Keep it that way. If it's not arched over, get it that way quickly by reeling up any slack, otherwise you don't need to work the reel right away. Hooked fish usually spend the first few seconds simply fighting the hook itself by tumbling and rolling, without really going anywhere.

In my experience, smaller fish of one or two pounds (0.5–1kg) simply keep this tumbling and rolling up until they wear down and get netted. As the fish tires, the pressure on the rod

alone gradually brings it closer. You simply have to keep the pressure on by keeping that rod bowed. Take up any slack by pump reeling. Don't reel in steadily. Instead, take in line as you drop the rod tip. Stop reeling as you pull the tip back up. Even when pump-reeling, keep a good bow in the rod. If the fish jumps. Let it. Don't make any special adjustments. Just keep the pressure on.

Bigger fish can be a little more challenging but you won't know this right away. In my experience, a 15in (39cm) fish feels about like a 30in (77cm) fish for the first few seconds or so. After that the smaller fish starts to tire quickly and you find yourself pumping it in. The bigger fish doesn't.

After an initial hook-fighting bout of tumbling and rolling, the bigger fish usually tries to leave the scene by running upstream or downstream. Downstream first, usually. If the drag is set right you don't need to do anything special. If the fish is strong enough – with some help by the current – it will take line. Let it. Don't panic. Remember, you've got at least

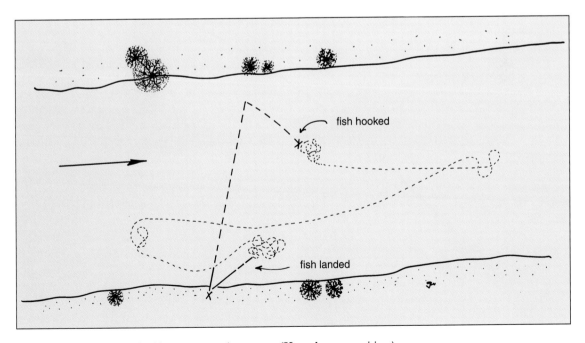

Typical running pattern of a bigger sea trout in current. (X marks your position.)

100yd (100m) of line. That's a whole football field. And 99 out of 100 fish will turn back upstream way before reaching that distance.

When it does turn, you've got to be ready. A big, strong sea trout can move upstream very quickly. If it's directly downstream it will be coming straight at you. You can't let it slacken the line. You've got to pump-reel quickly, enough to compensate and keep the bow in the rod. Here is where the fixed-spool reel with its high five-to-one gear ratio shows its worth.

Most big fish won't be tired yet and will swim right past you upstream. But usually not too far until it turns back toward you again, this time with the current behind it. This can be another hairy moment, which calls for frantic reeling. If you don't lose your head; if you keep pressure on the fish and be patient, then within a couple

of minutes your fish will be nearly played out and ready to be netted or beached.

One good trick to take the gas out of a big trout is to lead it into slack water. The oxygen density is lower in still than in running water, so the fish tires more quickly. That's also why, in my experience, fish hooked in still waters play out much sooner than in currents. Otherwise they tend to go through the same tumble-roll and run routines, so I play them the same.

Usually I don't need to mess with the drag setting when I'm playing a fish, but sometimes I do loosen it soon after I've set the hook to encourage the fish to run. I do this when I've hooked a fish very close to me. I find it's much harder to keep a freshly hooked, panic-stricken sea trout on a short line than a long one. So I loosen the drag just enough so that the fish is

Using the outboard to keep pressure on a fish.

free to run off some of its energy before I start pumping it in.

Playing Fish from a Boat

Playing a fish from a boat is a little trickier. I set the drag for the rod I'm holding the same as when I'm fishing from the bank, but I loosen the drag on any rod I'm fishing un-manned. That way a hard striker can take line until I can grab the rod and take control.

It's important to get any other lines (as well as downrigger or planer cables) reeled in and out of the way before dealing with a hooked fish. You also need to get the oars up. If there are two of you, this is a fairly easy operation. If you are alone, you've got to clear things up yourself before grabbing the live rod. Once you pick up the rod with the fish, reset the drag to normal, give it a good yank to make sure the hook is well set and play out the fish as you would from shore.

Obviously you are going to lose more fish on an un-manned rod than you would on the one you're holding when the fish strikes. Some anglers who fish alone feel the higher hook-up rate using two or even three rods outweighs the higher loss rate. Others don't and stick to fishing one rod.

On my local river anglers are also divided on how best to manoeuvre a harling boat when playing a fish. Some opt for pulling the oars or cutting the motor and letting the boat drift down-current while they play the fish. Others like myself like to keep the motor engaged. I find I can keep tension on the fish by manoeuvring the boat and working the throttle without having to work the reel. In either case you want to try to keep the fish at a safe distance from the boat until it's ready for netting; and at all costs keep it from running under the boat. If the fish is upstream when it takes, this can become tricky if and when it makes a downstream run. One solution is to pull the boat over toward the side, or even ground it near shore and play the fish out like you would on foot. Another is to move downstream with the fish. Different currents and levels of experience will determine which is best for you. On still waters it's mainly a question of keeping the fish out from under the boat. Some angler's keep the motor engaged so they can manoeuvre to do that.

Landing Sea Trout

Many experts say never try to land a sea trout until it's visibly spent and turning on its side. That's a good rule for bigger fish that you intend to keep. But if you are going to be returning a fish for any reason, it's best to get it landed quickly before it's completely exhausted to give it a better chance of recovering once it's back in the water.

If you are wading or fishing from the bank you've got two options for landing your fish: beaching it or netting it. If the bank is gradual, many anglers prefer to beach their fish because it avoids possible hang-ups with hooks getting caught in netting (below). To be beached safely a fish needs to be exhausted, so it's better to reserve beaching for the keepers.

Beaching Fish

To beach a fish, wait for it to turn on its side exhausted. Then guide it – with the rod still well bowed – steadily into the shallows and on to shore. With experience you'll make a mental note of good landing spots beforehand.

Most of the time, once the fish feels the bottom along its flanks, it will kick and strand itself further. Otherwise take hold of the tail wrist with thumb and forefinger and push it up on to shore. Don't try to lift it up by the tail like it's a salmon – you might lose it. Instead, take a good look at the hook-up. If it seems sound, drag the fish up away from the water with the still-bowed rod while pushing it up by the tail wrist.

What I do then is kneel down next to it, and before removing the hook, hold it firmly with my left hand and dispatch it with my right by knocking it on the head with a priest. I carry a sawed-off piece of hockey stick for this. If I can't get to it quickly enough, I use a cobble from the bank. It's only then that I remove the hook. To insure safe handling, I like to string the fish on to a short piece of nylon cord.

Beaching a sea trout.

Netting Fish

If the bank is high, or if you're fishing from a boat, netting is the only real option. There are lots of landing nets to choose from. Think about size and convenience. One with a 22–24in (56–62cm) diameter opening can handle most fish. For wading, a short-handled model with an elastic strap, so you can sling it across your back, works nicely. If you are mainly working from the bank or from a boat, models with longer handles of 6ft (2m) or so make landing much easier.

Single-piece nets are simple, strong and reliable. Many anglers favour these and I use one in my boat. But for wading and bank fishing I use a collapsible model with telescopic handle. It's a

ABOVE: A piece of hockey stick makes a light and effective priest.

RIGHT: A rucksack's-worth of gear for a day's outing: rod (in cloth case), collapsible landing net (in cloth case), lure box, Swiss Army knife (with hook file), thermometer, needle-nose pliers, dropper weights, extra spool (loaded), mono leader, priest, stringer, small first-aid kit, sandwich box, thermos.

little flimsier than the rigid models but I can fold it up and slide it into my rucksack next to my rod. For my next landing net, I've got my eye on Rapala's Guide Master.

Here are some basic rules for netting a sea trout:

1. Wait for a big fish to turn on its side before netting it. Smaller fish you can net sooner.
2. Sink the net down in the water first, then draw the fish over it. Be ready for a final burst of action once the fish sees the net.
3. Raise the net up around the fish from below. Big fish should go in head first if possible.

Netting a small fish.

The greatest risk when netting a fish is getting a hook caught on the outside of the netting. Even on good hook-ups, one or two points of a treble can be left exposed and can catch easily on the netting if you aren't careful. Obviously two and three-treble plugs are even more snag-prone, that's why you never want to try to scoop or swipe your net at a fighting fish. In my experience, the only thing to do when a fish hooks itself to the outside of the net is to grab the line and net and try to haul the whole thing up out of the water together.

You can minimize these risks when choosing netting. Unfortunately the tightly woven nylon-braid netting found on most models today is the most snag-prone. It's also harder to sweep through the water and it builds up ice so quickly that you might as well be using a colander!

Traditional models with a more open mesh of thinner line catch hooks less often and work more easily through the water. Models with stiffer plastic-line netting are also less problem prone, but harder to find.

Releasing Fish

If you want to release a fish you've netted, try to keep it wet and try not to handle it too much. It's best to keep the fish partially submerged in the net while removing the hook with needle nose pliers. If you can't get the hook out without causing major damage, it's better to cut the hook off and leave it in the fish. Chances are it will be expelled naturally.

Let the fish swim out of the net on its own, if it can. If it can't, cradle it gently with one hand under the pectoral fins while holding it by the tail wrist with the other. Move it back and forth gently to let oxygen circulate through the gills. Cradle it until it begins to swim away on its own.

Connections: Swivels and Leaders

Almost all spinning lures turn over or roll from time to time. Spoons roll as part of their natural action; plugs roll at higher speeds; even spinners roll very slowly when retrieved. This means you need a swivel connection somewhere to avoid twisting your line and causing all sorts of head-aches with tangles. The easiest route to go is the snap-swivel, and probably most spinners use them. They are simple and they let you change lures quickly. However, there are a couple of reasons why this isn't the best solution to line twist. First, snap-swivels tend to dampen the action of higher-action lures. Spoons and plugs need lots of freedom up front to go through their dart, wiggle, roll and wobble routines. Second, tying up directly to a swivel means a

break can occur anywhere up the line wherever there is a weak spot from wear and tear.

A much better way to go is with a swivel and leader (also called a trace or cast) set-up. Instead of a snap-swivel, you tie the lure directly to a leader with an open loop knot (*see* Knots below). Then you place the swivel about 2½–3½ft (0.75–1m) up the line. If the lure already comes with a swivel attached, remove that and use it. About the only time I use a snap-swivel is when I do want to dampen a spoon's action – say when I'm sweeping it through heavy currents or jigging it.

It's also a good idea to use a monofilament leader, and one of slightly lower breaking strength than the main line – especially when using braid for the main line. This ensures that any breaks occur between the swivel and lure rather than somewhere up the line. For casting presentations, simple barrel swivels work fine but when trolling or harling, ball-bearing swivels work better.

There is another reason to use the swivel and leader set-up: a swivel placed a little way up the

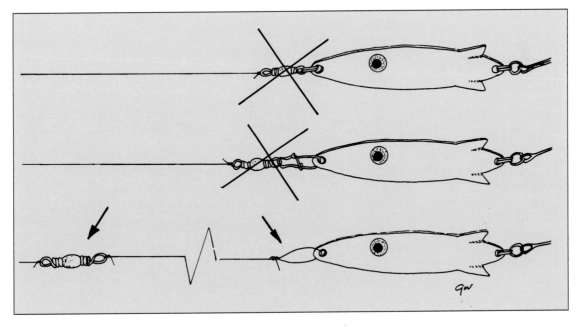

A leader-and-swivel set up makes the best connection to high action lures.

line can serve as an extra attractor to the lure. On many presentations the fish will catch sight of the swivel just before the lure. The swivel works as a heads-up call. Don't think of it as something to camouflage. Think of it as a way to bring attention to your lure. Swivels come in different finishes, like silver, copper, gold, even colours. Some anglers think about visibility when choosing swivels like they do for spoons and spinners.

Ledger Rigs

Lots of spin-anglers shy away from fishing with ledgers (sinkers). They worry about ruining a

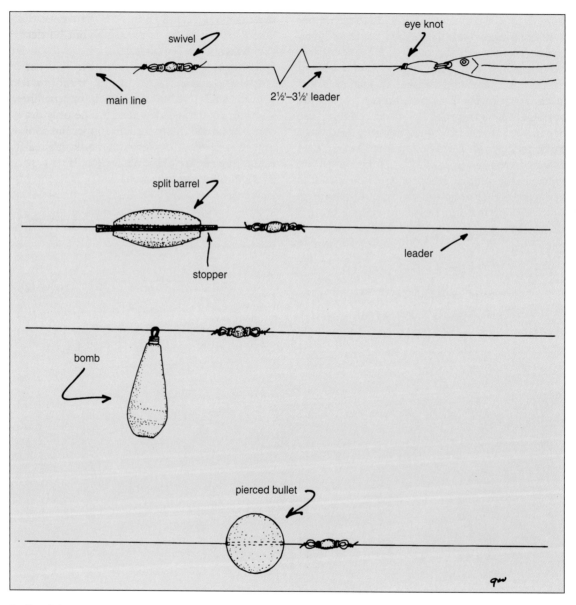

In-line sinkers.

lure's action. There's no need, if you rig them up correctly. Ledger rigs let you get your lure where you otherwise couldn't – that's efficiency! Buoyant lures, like plugs, are usually fished off ledger rigs; so are flutter-spoons, and sometimes even lighter casting spoons. You've got several options here: in-line and dropper-weight rigs

In-Line Sinkers

First, in-lines are easier to rig up: you simply add the sinker just above the swivel on your standard swivel-leader set-up. The in-line rig is also easier to cast and a little less prone to tangling than a dropper. However, in-lines make it harder to keep a non-floating lure grazing bottom without hanging up, than with a dropper set-up. So, I tend to use an in-line rig when working a non-floating lure high in the water, or when fishing deep along a less snag-prone bottom of, say, sand or small gravel.

As for types of in-lines, there are plenty to choose from: you've got split shot, pierced ball, bomb, split-barrel with stopper and Wye types. I don't like split shot, which you squeeze on the line with pliers, because I can't remove or change them very easily. A pierced ball or bomb that you string on the line works OK, but sometimes it rides up the line when you're casting, which makes for some unsettling seconds until it seats itself back down on to the swivel. The Wye type is nearly problem-free, but harder to find outside the British Isles.

My favourite in-line sinker is the split-barrel with stopper. You can get this on or off in a few seconds and you don't need to cut or retie lines. You can reposition it easily too. The only drawback is you end up losing the stopper pin sooner or later. If you are on the bank it's easily replaced with a small twig of wood. If you are in a boat you can be in trouble.

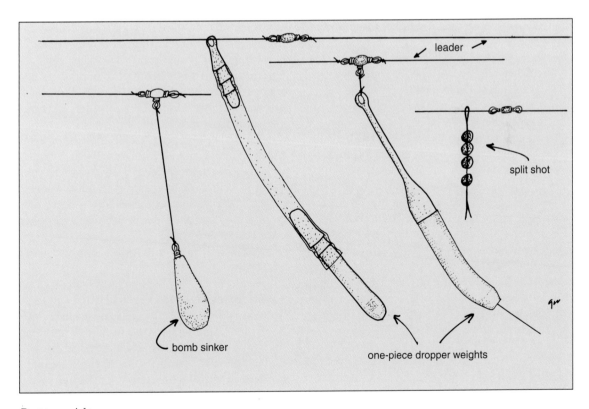

leader

split shot

bomb sinker

one-piece dropper weights

Dropper-weights.

It's usually recommended that the weight of the in-line sinker not exceed that of the lure itself, or else the lure will wrap back on the main line when you are casting. I violate this rule all the time when I'm casting flutter-spoons. I usually get away with it.

Dropper-Weights

Dropper or paternoster rigs are harder to cast, more tangle-prone and dampen the feel of your lure's action more than in-line rigs. They are also a little more involved to rig up, but for working over very snaggy bottoms with heavier spoons and spinners, it's worth it. You can bounce the weight along the bottom and know your lure will be trailing a safer distance up off the bottom.

Dropper-weights also vary. Most anglers simply use a bomb sinker connected to a three-way or tee-swivel by a short, say, ½ft (15cm) piece of mono, sometimes called a bomb-link rig. A weaker break-strength mono is used on the dropper line, so only the sinker is lost if they can't free a snag. Another option is pinching split shot to a short dropper line.

There are also one-piece dropper-weights. The simpler one is a piece of flexible, clear plastic tubing with lead or tungsten in one end and an eye in the other. You can string it right on the main line above the swivel, or tie it to the tee-swivel with weaker strength mono so it will break away when hopelessly snagged. Another model with an even better design has a flexible steel needle protruding from the bottom of the weight itself, which helps it bump along even the snaggiest bottoms without much trouble.

In my experience bomb-link rigs are a better choice for upstream harling and light trolling because they have less resistance than the one-piece variety. For casting, I like the one-piece dropper because it hangs up less on the bottom.

Leader Length

As for leader length, between 2½–3½ft (0.75–1m) of mono is usual, depending on water clarity and type of lure you are using. Bear in mind when ledgering, that non-buoyant lures like casting spoons tend to run deeper off a longer leader, but buoyant lures higher. You'll need to experiment to get the right combinations.

A final note: watch out for any restrictions on using lead. More and more waters are banning lead under a certain weight, usually around 1oz (c. 28g). It's not a matter of water pollution (lead is pretty inert in clean water) but to save waterfowl. Small lead shot and sinkers sometimes get swallowed by foraging water birds. The toxic lead sits in the crop and eventually poisons them. The solution is easy, just use non-toxic weights, which are now widely available in most shapes and sizes.

Lines, Rods and Reels

Over the years I have used many different combinations of lines, rods and reels for presenting lures to sea trout, as well as salmon. I can remember really good days using spliced-together lines I found along the bank, or a rod snapped off to two-thirds its original size, even a reel that just wouldn't turn about half the time. I've also had week-long slumps with perfect tackle. So this means tackle doesn't matter much, right? Wrong. It's still much easier to pull off the presentations you need to when your outfit is well co-ordinated and in good working order. The right tackle makes you a more efficient angler and that means more sea trout per day over the long run.

First, which lines, rods and reels will work best?

Lines: Monofilament versus Braid Lines

Spinning lines have changed a lot since Jock Scott and Hugh Falkus wrote about spinning for sea trout. Nylon monofilaments are much better now and we also have a whole range of impressive high-tech braids (sometimes called super- or fusion-lines) to choose from. Both have their pluses and minuses.

Tip: Soak Mono Before Use

You can reduce the risk of new monofilament line springing off the drum of a fixed-spool reel by soaking the loaded spool in hot tap-water for a few minutes before you use it.

Monofilament

Mono is easier to handle and much cheaper than super-line, and because mono is more flexible or stretchy, it's easier to keep pressure on a hooked fish than with the less stretchy braid, especially when a fish is jumping or rushing right at you. I have already noted that mono makes better leaders because it is more resistant to wear and tear than braid. Using a mono leader of a somewhat lower break-strength than the main line also helps ensure that any breakage will occur at the terminal knots, rather than way up the line. Finally, a mono leader also acts as a kind of shock-absorber for a main line of braid.

On the down side, mono, because it is stretchy, is less sensitive to what's going on at the lure end, than is braid. With mono it's much harder to feel the lure's action – whether it's fluttering too fast or slow, whether it's tapping the bottom, whether it's picked up weeds, even whether a fish has quietly taken it. It's also harder to set the hook quickly with mono. Mono also loses a lot of its flexibility in sub-zero temperatures, the result being that it tends to want to jump off the drum unless you keep it under constant tension.

Braids

Braid line on the other hand is extremely sensitive to terminal events. It lets you keep more precise and accurate control over your presentation, and allows you to respond more quickly to a strike. And because braid is stronger than mono, you can use a thinner line that cuts through the water more easily, again adding better lure control. Braid's relatively smaller diameter also allows you to cast the same lure farther than you can with mono. Finally, whereas mono sinks, most braids float, which is a great help when drifting a lure or mending line on a sweep.

Braid's drawbacks include greater difficulty in keeping pressure on a jumping or charging fish, a greater tendency to carry water into the rod guides and reel, which means more problems with icing-up in winter, and braid is much less resistant to abrasion than mono. Even a small fraying from contact with rocks renders it very vulnerable to breakage. And braid is much more tangle-prone than mono.

Braid's relative brittleness, coupled with its lack of stretch, has led some away from using it when trolling. They argue that mono absorbs the shock of a strike from a big sea trout better than braid does. So, again, we need to make some trade-offs. But remember, whichever line you use, keep track of its condition, especially the last metre or so, where it has been bouncing off rocks or ice, and at the knots, especially when using the less abrasion-resistant braids. When I'm fishing braid over an abrasive bottom, I use an extra long leader of tougher mono ($3\frac{1}{2}$–$6\frac{1}{2}$ft or 1–2m). Don't forget also that both mono and braid quickly lose strength under ice-water conditions, especially after being stressed by a fish or a bottom snag. So it pays to check line-strength with a serious pull after a snag, a played fish or any time you change a lure.

How Strong a Line?

Maybe the biggest question facing the sea-trout spin-angler is what gauge line to use. Strength is usually the first thought, 'Can it handle my dream fish?'. Fair enough but if you look at catch statistics you'll find that the size of your typical catch will run to about 2lb (1kg) more or less, depending on where you fish. A five-pounder (2.5kg) gets photographed, anything over 10lb (4.5kg) gives you bragging rights, anything over twenty (9kg) wins you prizes. Sea trout are beautiful, exciting and hard fighters, but very few reach the monster-sizes reported from some Danish beats. Most sea trout that you are going to have the fortune of hooking during a lifetime will be easily handled on lines of up to 20lb (9kg) test. If you are fishing in one of those rarer places known to have really big fish, you can bump up the gauge.

Within those limits, your choice of lines will depend in part on whether you believe sea trout are what the old time fliers call 'gut shy' or not. Traditional wisdom in the British Isles seems to say that sea trout do react negatively if they can see the line. So the custom there is to go with thinner lines when the water is low and clear (called low-water or light spinning) and somewhat thicker lines when the water is high and coloured (called high-water or heavy spinning). For light spinning, authors like Jock Scott, Falkus, Harris and Morgan, and Bingham suggest mono with break-strengths of 4–10lb (2–4.5kg), with slightly lighter leaders; and for heavy spinning, 8–12lb (3.6–5.5kg) break-strength (also with lighter leaders).

In contrast, both in Scandinavia and North America the feeling is that sea trout don't care too much about line thickness, at least up to c. 20lb (9kg) break-strength (c. 0.30mm diameter) monofilament. It's felt that sea trout focus on the lure and not the line, and that line should be chosen mainly with performance in mind.

Unfortunately there are no scientific studies that I know of to settle the issue of whether sea trout are 'gut shy' or not. I tend to rank performance over visibility when choosing line. Ask yourself, 'Is it strong enough to play a fish firmly and land it quickly in case I want to release it?', 'Does it float or sink?', 'Can I cast the lures I want to far enough?', 'Is it sensitive enough to control the presentation?', 'Does it allow me to set the hook quickly?', 'Is it strong enough to land a dream fish or retrieve a snagged lure?'.

Matching Line with Rod

Some of the drawbacks with both mono and braid lines can be minimized by choosing high-quality line and by making the right rod match. If you are going to be fishing mainly monofilament, then you should opt for a rod with a fairly stiff action. This will compensate for monofilament's relative insensitivity, enhance feel and so, lure control. If you are going to be fishing mainly braid, then think about a softer action rod. It will compensate for the braids inflexibility and give your tackle a little more give when playing a fish.

Rod length should also be chosen with feel and control in mind. Longer rods let you cast farther but require more room. Shorter rods are easier to use when you've got limited space, like along a wooded stream bank or in a small boat, but they won't cast a lure as far as a longer rod will. Whichever you choose, make sure it can handle weights up to $1\frac{3}{8}$oz (40g). This should be printed right on the rod shaft.

Here are some recommended line and rod combinations:

river casting/harling: 8–9ft rod, 10–30lb test line;

surf/still-water casting: 8–10ft rod, 8–12lb test line;

river/still-water ice-fishing: $2\frac{1}{2}$–4ft rod, 8–12lb test line;

light trolling: 8–9ft rod, 10–20lb test line.

Reels

I think if you took a survey of hardware anglers who fish for sea trout you'd probably find about half using fixed-spool reels (classic spinning reels) and about half using multipliers (classic level-wind or bait-casting reels). Some of this reflects informed choice but much of it doesn't. For one thing, some believe the multiplier symbolizes experience and great skill: you start out with a fixed-spool then you graduate to a level-wind. That's pure fallacy. At least where I fish, choice doesn't correspond to skill. While many master spin-anglers do use level-winds, many others use fixed-spool reels. The fact is, each kind of reel does some things better. Your choice of reel – if you are going to own only one – should be based on the kind of spinning you're likely to be doing most of the time. If you can afford two set-ups, even better: then you can change as required. In either case, here are few of the strengths and weaknesses of each.

Fixed-spool reels cast lighter lures farther and more easily than multipliers. Multipliers cast heavier lures as well as fixed-spool reels but suffer problems with backlash. Multipliers are stronger than fixed-spool reels, have better drag systems and probably last longer. Fixed-spool reels need less room to cast effectively and accurately, but with a multiplier you can feed line out more quickly and easily. Multipliers are more expensive than fixed-spool reels.

Before choosing a reel think about your typical application. If you normally fish heavily wooded small to medium-sized rivers, where you will be tossing mainly light lures from cramped surroundings, then the fixed-spool is probably your best bet. If you are fishing mainly larger rivers, open waters with plenty of room to cast heavier lures or trolling, then the multiplier might be a better choice. If you are putting together an outfit for ice-fishing only, then look for a miniature fixed-spool or multiplier designed for it.

Whichever reel you choose, try to get the very best you can afford. Look for models that are simple and easy to use. The more ball-bearings the better. Find models where the drag lever is quickly accessible. The spool or drum should be able to hold at least 150yd (150m) of line. On fixed-spool reels make sure the spool is interchangeable and keep a backup loaded. As far as quality, Shimano, Daiwa and Abu probably set today's standards for both multiplier and fixed-spool models.

Knots

I once lost a nice fish because a knot pulled loose. It took me all day to recover. Now I think more about how my rig is tied together. You don't need to know a lot of knots – only the right ones. Here are some good choices.

What I Use

Personally, in monofilaments I like Berkeley Trilene Sensation. It is about as sensitive as mono can be – enough to keep me in touch with the lure during most presentations – and still stretchy enough to keep pressure on a hooked fish. It is also very strong and powerful for its diameter. When it comes to braids, I like Power Pro. Apart from being extremely strong for its diameter, it is wonderfully sensitive. It also has a little flex, which helps when playing fish.

I could probably improve my performance if I used two rods – a stiffer action one for the mono and a softer action one for braid – but I like simplicity, so I use one fairly stiff-action, 9ft (270cm) Shimano Catana with a ½–1⅜oz (15–40g) casting-weight-rating for both mono and braid, and I have no complaints. My reel is a Shimano 4000 series with twin handle for fast pick up, reverse brake, easily accessible quick-action rear drag and interchangeable drums, which can carry around 150yd (150m) of 0.35mm mono and over 300 of 0.19mm braid. I use this rig on most types of water for sea trout, and have also taken many salmon on it up to 25lb (11kg) size.

Loop or Rapala Knot

This is the knot to use for attaching spoons or diving plugs to the leader so you don't cramp their action. It's very easy to tie and strong. Remember to make four turns before you bring it back through the eye.

Trilene Knot

This is the best knot for typing mono to a swivel or a sinker or to any lure you aren't worried about dampening the action of, like a spinner. It's strong and easy to tie – even in a rocking boat. It's the only one I use but a

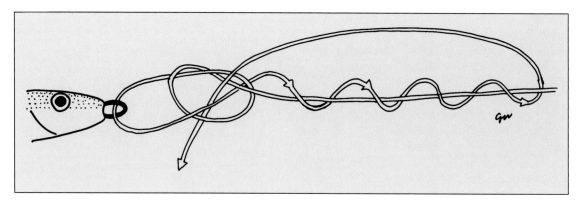

Loop or Rapala knot.

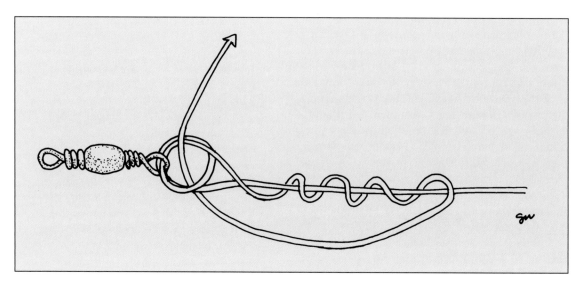

Trilene knot.

decent alternative is the more traditional tucked half-blood or clinch knot. Make four turns on each.

Double-Tucked Half-Blood and Double-Trilene Knots

Braids are very slippery due to their coatings. If you tie them the same as you do mono, you risk them pulling loose. The best way to keep knots in these lines tight is to wet them first before tying them and then to use either a double-tucked half-blood or double-trilene knot. I like the double-trilene because you end up with four loops through the eye, which makes the knot more abrasion-resistant.

Double-Grinner Knot

You don't want to splice two lines together if you can help it but, if you have to, the best way to do it is with a double-grinner. It's stronger than the blood knot but takes more practice to tie quickly. I find it helps to think of it as two

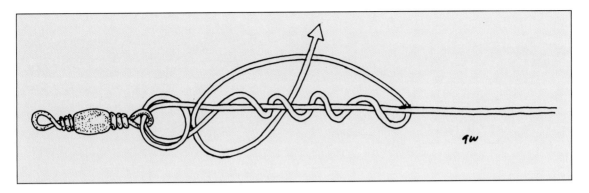

Double-tucked half-blood knot.

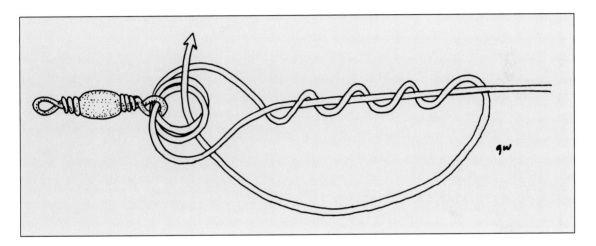

Double-trilene knot.

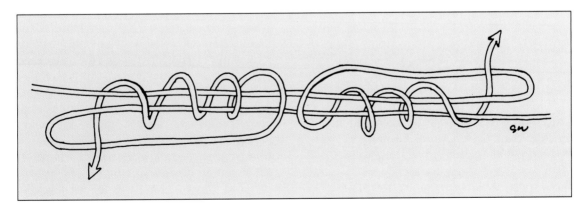

Double-grinner knot.

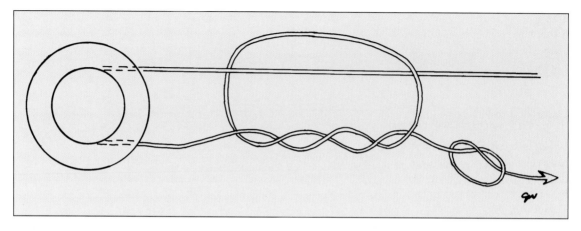

Mono-reel knot.

knots and then to tie each separately. Remember to make four turns on each.

Mono-Reel Knot

Don't wait to think about how you've tied your line to the reel drum until a big sea trout is stripping off your last yard! The reel knot is your final link, so you need to make it a good one. For tying monofilament directly to the drum, use the mono-reel knot, which has a knotted free end to prevent slippage. Make four turns on the main part. Braids are prone to slide around the drum if tied directly to it, so if you are using braid for the main line, tie it first to a few feet (1m) of mono by a double-grinner knot, then attach the mono to the drum with the mono-reel knot.

Wading and Waders

Catch sight of a angler waist-high in mid-stream and you think fly-fisherman. Look again. More and more spin-angler's are wearing waders, and there are some good reasons for it. Casting room is one. Although spinning doesn't take as much space as flying, on heavily wooded streams it's simply much easier to hit your target water when you can wade out from under overhanging branches. Positioning is another. When casting from the water your lure spends more time in currents where sea trout hold, and less time in slack water where they don't. Wading also gets you closer to the target water and it allows you to cover it with a shorter line so that you've got better control.

How deep you wade depends on how strong the current is and how secure the footing. Some like to work thigh-deep, others chest-deep. Hugh Falkus argued that if you are going to wade, then wade carefully and wade deep, since a low-profile on the water is less likely to spook a fish than a tall one on the bank.

Waders are standard gear along the coast, where wading out gives you the extra distance you need to get your lure beyond the weed beds or into deeper holding water. For wading in smaller streams, many anglers get by with old-fashioned thigh waders, but for river and coastal fishing, chest-high models are more useful. Both can be found in traditional PVC rubber and in newer high-tech materials incorporating Gore Tex or similar membranes to make them breathable. You can get them in one piece or with separate boots. If you are going to be fishing right through the winter, you'll need to go with thicker ⅕in (4–5mm) Neopren waders for full comfort. Plenty of companies make the full range. Check at the local tackle shop to see what the locals are wearing.

Using Stealth

By all accounts sea trout are easily alarmed – maybe more so than other trout or salmon. Old-timers say you can stimulate a salmon to strike by agitating it (splashing, throwing rocks in the water) but not a sea trout! A spooked or wary sea trout may or may not flee, but it won't strike a lure. 'Agitate salmon to bite/calm sea trout to bite', is the old saying.

We've already seen how sea trout use vision, 'hearing' via the lateral line, and smell to detect the presence of prey. We can't forget that they use these same senses to detect predators, like us! To have any chance of scoring with sea trout we have to fish undetected. That calls for stealth.

Staying out of sight, especially if the water is still and clear, is a start. Sea trout may be near-sighted but they are also extremely good at detecting movements and contrast. So, take it slow. Stay down and watch your background. Don't make a point of standing out. Personally, I don't go the full route and wear camouflage, but I don't wear light clothes against a dark background, or dark clothes in snow either. Always work the near water first before wading in. Cast a long line – literally 'cast out of sight' – and on smaller flows approach your target water from downstream when you can.

As for light levels, it's not full daylight you need to worry about as much as dusk, dawn, moon-lit nights and those grey cloudy days when sea trout see at their best. Stay down and don't cast shadows over your target water, whether on foot or in your boat. Actually full sunlight on the water makes it hard for trout to see much above the water at all. It has to do with the effects of reflection and refraction of light.[49] From the trout's point of view, looking up is like looking into a mirror, except for a window of about 45 degrees directly overhead, where the view of things above the surface is clearer. The window is bigger when the fish is deep and smaller when it's higher up. Obviously, you want to stay outside that window. That's why it's often better to wade deeply.

Avoiding vibrations is even more important. Sea trout probably can't 'hear' much of what's going on above the water. So talking, even hollering, to mates down the bank or in another boat probably isn't going to spook them, but anything that causes underwater vibrations surely will. Stumbling along the bank, clumsy wading, stomping and banging around inside the boat are all going to put fish on the alert. Trollers don't agree on whether the sound of a boat's motor spooks sea trout but experienced harlers pad the oar locks to muffle the sound of rowing.

Most anglers pay little attention to smell unless they are using bait. Yet, smell probably does help sea trout detect and avoid certain predators like bears, otters, seals, maybe humans. Hugh Falkus felt that the odour of an injured fish could produce a fright reaction among a shoal of sea trout, and Bernie Taylor describes some research by scientists at Pure Fishing that found a list of scents that seemed to repel trout. These included sunscreen, insect repellent, certain cosmetic fragrances, nicotine from tobacco, even the alcohol you find in towelettes and waterless washes.[50] So, at the very least it's a good idea to wash you hands before handling your fishing gear. If you are wading, keep you boots clean from obvious contaminants like those listed. Some trout anglers go one further by covering their own scent. Light oil like WD40, believe it or not, seems to work. Or try smearing your hands with attractants like fish oil, or crushed shrimp, or artificials like powerbait. It can't hurt, and might help.

4 TACTICAL GUIDE FOR ALL WATERS AND SEASONS

So far, we've taken a close look at what makes a good sea-trout lure, put together a tool-kit of types we can feel confident in and scoped-out a range of presentations. Now it's time to put all this together into something useful at waterside. We want a set of tactical guidelines to help decide which lures and presentations will give us the best shot at taking sea trout under all the different conditions we are likely to encounter on the water.

Thinking Tactically

A good place to start is thinking about the kinds of information you'll need to make tactical decisions. The first thing to decide is what type of water or waters you will be fishing. I've grouped them below into five categories, which should pretty much cover the range: rivers, tailwaters, brackish estuaries, salt-water coastlines and freshwater lakes.

Next you'll need to determine the conditions you'll be fishing under. Most anglers think in terms of season. That's alright, but don't get hung up on dates. Seasons change at different times in different places. Instead, think about seasons in terms of conditions that affect sea-trout taking behaviour, like water temperature, turbidity and light levels. It's a common mistake to fish by the calendar instead of the conditions. In my area, come every 1 May light-trolling boats start to appear in the estuary. Some of these boats fish the same way every year, regardless: they troll spoons high and fast in hopes of taking sea trout that are hunting schools of spawning smelts. Some years they do well. Some years not. Problem is: water in early May

is often barely over 42°F (5°C). Sea trout are still sitting in a cold stupor in winter lies near the bottom, and have little interest in lures whizzing 6ft (2m) above their heads. A simple reading of the water temperature would have clued these anglers into going after those cold fish with something deep and slow – they might have taken a few home. Instead, they get weeks of trolling practice until the water and the fish warm up to their speed – not very efficient, not very tactical.

Asking Yourself Questions

A tactical approach calls for first determining the conditions you are dealing with; then dealing with them as best you can. You can start by asking yourself a few questions – even before thinking about which lure you should use or how you should present it.

What is the Water Temperature?

First question, and probably the most important, what is the water temperature? Carry a good thermometer and use it often. I carry one with me even when I'm not fishing, so that I can check my local river whenever I'm nearby. Remember, the ideal range for sea trout is between 47 and 56°F (8–13°C). Outside this range and both the trout and you will need to make adjustments.

You probably remember from chemistry class that when water drops below 40°F (4°C) it starts getting lighter.[51] No? Well, it means that in freezing water – especially when it's still – it can be warmer near the bottom, so that's where the fish will be!

Take note also whether the air is much warmer or colder than the water temperature. A

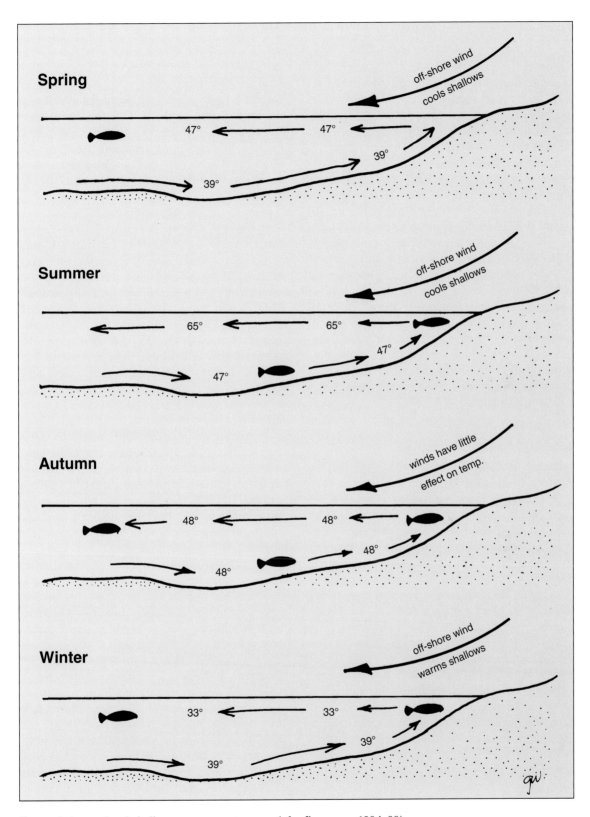

Spring

off-shore wind
cools shallows

47° 47° 39°

39°

Summer

off-shore wind
cools shallows

65° 65°

47°

47°

Autumn

winds have little
effect on temp.

48° 48°

48°

48°

Winter

off-shore wind
warms shallows

33° 33°

39°

39°

Seasonal changes in wind effects on water temperature (after Joergensen 1994–99).

cold snap, or a rapid drop of night air temperature on warmer water can 'put-fish-down', i.e. drive them into a temporary state of lethargy until they have adjusted to the change. A rapid drop in the barometer, like before a rain storm, can have the same effect.[52]

And don't forget the effects of wind on water temperature, especially if you are fishing open water in a lake or estuary or along the coast. An on-shore wind usually warms the shallows, while an off-shore cools them. Unless the water is under 40°F (4°C), then it has the opposite effect!

During spring and summer an off-shore wind cools the shallows by blowing warmer surface water out and drawing cooler, deeper water in. During the autumn, after water is well mixed, winds have little effect on water temperature. During a cold winter an off-shore wind may actually warm the shallows because deeper and warmer water will be drawn inshore, and fish will be drawn with it.

How Clear is the Water?
You'll also want to get an idea of water clarity or turbidity. How far can you see through it? Can you see the bottom? Wade in. Can you still see your boot tips when waist-deep? Can you see even deeper? Not that deep? Toss in a lure and see how far it sinks before you lose sight of it. Remember, the distance you can see through the water is always much greater than the distance a near-sighted sea trout will react to your lure. This is also a good opportunity to see whether your lure looks the way you want it to. Right action? Brightness? Visibility?

How About the Water Surface?
Is the water dead calm and flat? Rippled? Choppy? Rough? Sea trout are shy and don't like to feel exposed, so a broken surface almost always fishes better than a glassy calm one. A little wind, some current, even a rain that breaks the surface can make all the difference in your quarry's willingness to take a lure.

How Light Is It?
How about light level? Is it normal, bright

daylight? Is it dawn, dusk or is the sky heavily overcast? Is it night? Different light conditions call for different methods. Full sun often fishes best in the dead of winter, subdued light best in spring and fall, and darkness best in the summer. Bigger fish tend to feed from dusk 'till dawn, smaller fish more opportunistically. Schedule accordingly.

How High is the Water?
Water level is also important. In rivers and tail-waters, dirty water usually coincides with high water, clear water with low – but not always, so check it out. Does the current seem normal and steady? Does it seem high? Is it flowing fast and high on the banks, or flooding the shallows and inlets? Does it seem low? Is it lying more or less still in its bed? Is it falling? Rising?

Watching familiar water over time you'll get a feel for these changes. You can also check a water-level gauge if you can find one. They are often on bridges, or you can make a visual mark on some feature like a boulder and check water level against it periodically. Also check the bank or rocks for wetness, and for surface tension of the water where it comes into contact with these features. If it is sagging that means falling water. If it is bulging, then the water is rising.

In tidal waters you'll want to keep track of the current's direction. Is it moving up (flowing) or down (ebbing) the estuary? Is it moving up or down or diagonally along the beach? This can clue you into where fish are likely to be and what they will be doing. Get hold of a good tide table so you can plan to be there when conditions are best for finding takers.

What Are My Targets?
Now, once you've established basic conditions on your particular piece of water, think about your best targets. Ask yourself, where are sea trout most likely to be holding? I've made some recommendations below based on general knowledge, but don't overlook any immediate clues either. Flashes near the bottom can mean drift-feeding trout, so can surface splashes. How about bait fish? Are they darting around near

Water level gauges: look for them on bridge pilings, like here.

the shore? Maybe sea trout are hunting nearby. Sometimes from your boat you can see schools of bait fish fleeing sea trout near the surface. Other predators usually join the fray like gulls, terns, loons, osprey, diving duck, herons, etc., so watch for them too. And don't forget to keep an eye on other anglers. If they are clustering along the beach or in their boats they are probably working over a temporary hotspot. Think about joining them!

Which Lures and Presentations Should I Use?
Now you can think about which lures and presentations to use. You've got plenty to choose from. Think in terms of which lure action, size, brightness, colour and pattern is most likely to elicit a strike given the prevailing conditions (regardless of the month). Think about which presentations are more likely to get that lure in the sea-trout's strike zone. This will depend on whether you are fishing on foot or from a boat, in still water or a current. I've made some recommendations for each. Start with these, then experiment with others.

Keeping a Journal
Good tactics are built up from long experience. Over the years patterns emerge. You see correlations between factors like water type, temperature, clarity, light levels, presentation and the size, shape and pattern of the lures you use. In time you see what works under some conditions and not others. But, unless you have a photographic memory, a lot of useful information gets forgotten. I can probably remember what the water temperature was the last time I was out, but how about last 15 April when I took that four-pounder on the river? Not a chance. But I know I can find it easy enough – I just dig it out of my journal.

Most serious sea-trouters keep some sort of journal to record their experiences. It doesn't have to be a literary masterpiece, just a record of the relevant facts, so you can refer to it later. To be really useful it should record not only the good days, but the blanks too. That's the only way you'll ever know which factors have been important to success (*see* box).

Keeping a journal

The entries in a journal might include the following:

- Date
- Time
- Fish hooked/ landed/ killed/released
- Catch weight and length
- Catch sex
- Catch condition (kelt, spawning adult, etc.)
- Stomach contents (empty, fish, insects, etc.)
- Type of water (river, lake, estuary, coastline, etc.)
- Section or beat (pool, run, flats, bridge, etc.)
- Water and air temperatures (as measured)
- Water clarity/visibility (10ft or 3m, <3ft or <1m, etc.)

- Water surface (smooth, broken, etc.)
- Water current/height (heavy, low, flooding, ebbing, etc.)
- Lighting/weather (low light, bright sunlight, dawn, dusk, moonlit night, overcast, etc.)
- Wind speed and direction (hard, light, on-shore, off-shore, up-river, down-river)
- Lure (size/weight, type, pattern)
- Presentation and rigging (e.g. deep-drift, high sweep, deep-troll, flat-line, dropper-weight, downrigger, diver, planer, etc.)
- Lure/trolling speed (fast, medium, slow, 1kn, 3kn, etc.)
- You can add, modify or delete entries to fit the kinds of fishing you normally do.

A journal is a good way to build know-how over the long run. It also lets you track your performance over the years.

Now for tactics.

Tactics for Rivers

Probably more sea trout are taken in rivers than anywhere else. Learning to be successful on these waters is mainly a matter of learning how seasonal changes in water level, water temperature and water clarity affect where sea trout are going to be at any moment and what they are most likely to respond to in the way of lures and presentations.

Spring River Tactics

On many rivers spring is when the new sea trout season begins. For spin-anglers it's a time for new challenges and great opportunities. Unless it has been a very mild winter, larger rivers will be carrying at least two sorts of sea trout: spawned-out kelts and fatter sea trout that have over-wintered in freshwater. Both will be making their way downstream toward summer ranges in the salt and both will be eating voraciously as the water warms up. Some rivers will also receive early runs of sea trout: both mature spawning sea trout and younger fish called 'finnock'.[54] The finnock may or may not spawn, but they often keep feeding actively, so these are also good targets.

The main challenges on spring rivers are finding and covering fish in water that is almost always much higher and more turbid than at other times. However, these same conditions can also mean some of the best sea-trouting has to offer for the spin-angler. Fish become more active as water temperatures move into the ideal range between 47 and 56°F (8–13°C). Turbidity provides added security, so sea trout feel less edgy, move around a lot more freely and hunt more actively than at other times, even during the day.

Finding the best way to target spring sea trout will depend on just how high and turbid the current becomes. Many northern rivers carry heavy flows from melting ice and snow for much of the spring. In regions with mainly rainy springs, like the famous spate rivers of the British Isles, water levels can fluctuate from flood to more or less normal levels right through spring and summer. Let's look at heavy-water tactics first.

Fishing Heavy Spring Flows

When rivers run very high and fast, sea trout take refuge from the strongest currents. Now you'll find them holding station in the seams where slacker water meets the main currents, in the slower water near the bank, under roots and over-hanging bushes or trees, in the slower water of a pool tail, around islands, bridges, large boulders and other structures that break the flow, and in the little bays that form off the main stream. Fish will avoid whirlpools, but big back-eddies are also prime holds in very heavy water. Remember, fish always face into the current, so those holding in a big back-eddy will be facing downriver. These are the places you'll need to target if you want to score in heavy water.

Turbidity is another factor. High water is usually coloured water where visibility is typically under 3ft (1m). That means our targets will have an effective strike zone of less than 2ft (60cm).

As for tactics, these conditions call for a lure that can easily be detected in dirty water and presentations that can keep it in the strike zone long enough to be grabbed before our fish loses sight of it. So slower is better.

NEAR-SHORE STRIP

On heavy flows, the near-shore strip will hold most of the fish and that should be your main target water. The best way to cover it is probably backing-down, hanging and stop-and-go. It doesn't need to be a heavy lure because the water isn't that deep and you want to be able to suspend it in the flow. You'll want something big with a strong pattern to make it visible. A swimming spoon would be my first choice. A big

ABOVE: River in high water. BELOW: Covering heavy spring flows. (X marks your position.)

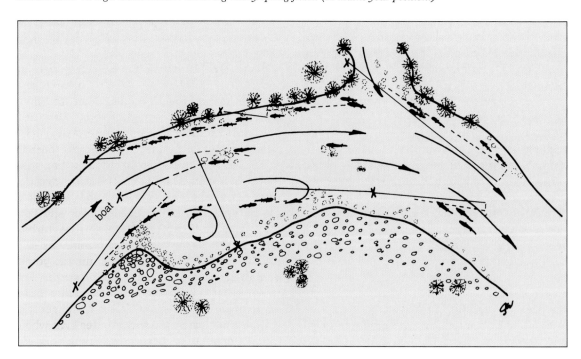

noisy spinner would be my second choice. If the current isn't too strong, you might even give a ledgered flutter-spoon a try. Patterns with fluorescent red, orange and yellow are good choices. To increase efficiency, I like to wade out, if the current isn't too strong, to a position in the taking strip directly upstream. This way I can work the lure down and up slowly and hang it in the current as long as I want, before moving downstream to work the next piece of the strip.

OTHER TARGET WATERS

Covering targets further out from the bank is harder but it is usually worth a try, especially if you are going for trophies, since it is the bigger and stronger fish that can defend these choice refuges in the deeper, stronger currents. Roll-ledgering a high-speed, strong-pattern flutter-spoon or lighter swimming spoon is probably your best move. Or try sweeping a large, heavy swimming or jigging spoon on a long line. Working from a position well above your target water lets you keep your spoon working slowly on a diagonal crossing pattern through the target.

You can also try drifting a spoon down through a seam in the channel, or into calmer pockets further out. I find it's nearly impossible to keep a drift spoon fishing deep when working across stronger currents. When I do manage it, the spoon is drifting too fast to be effective anyway.

Another possibility is using a boat.

HARLING

Harling from a moving boat in very high currents becomes an issue of control, if not safety. Most of the time it's not worth the trouble or risk, but working from an anchored boat can be. With the right positioning you can back-down and hang lures in choice holding water you'd otherwise have to cover by sweeping or drifting from the bank.

NIGHT FISHING

Because low visibility and a small strike-zone become big factors when fishing heavy, turbid water, your best chances for scoring are going to come during full daylight, from after dawn to before dusk. If you want to try fishing in lower light, bear in mind that you are targeting a quarry with near-zero reaction distance. If so, I'd suggest concentrating on the near-shore strip. You can fish it a couple of ways. First, you can try backing-down and hanging the same lures you used in full daylight, or you can try dragging a big, dark, wake-lure in the current. Remember you are trying to attract fish by the lure's wake, so keep it fishing at the surface. You might also want to give those lures you painted with glo-paint a try. If you've ever considered tipping your hooks with something smelly like shrimp or squid, now's the time.

Fishing Normal Spring Flows

On most rivers by late spring, water has returned to near-normal flow levels and cleared up to a semi-opaque colour with visibility anywhere from 3 to 6ft (1–2m). This is the 'pale lager beer or very weak coffee' water the experts write about. Since the water temperature is still under 56°F (13°C), and coloured enough so that sea trout feel secure, these are nearly ideal taking conditions for the spin-angler. To make the most of them you'll need to cover the water a little differently than you did when the flow was heavier.

First, many fish won't be where they were in higher water. They still won't be occupying their normal clear low-water holds. Once the flow subsides and visibility reaches about 3ft (1m), then sea trout will leave those near-shore high-water refuges and spread out across deeper water. The key to taking them is covering that water thoroughly. The best way to do that on foot is to work to a grid. Remember to keep a tight spacing between casts to cover any fish present. Even though the slightly less turbid conditions means a bigger strike zone, it's still only 1½–2½ft (45–75cm) maximum, so you'll need to get your lure close to elicit a strike.

Now that water clarity and visibility have improved, the best time to fish is no longer full daylight but during periods of lower light when fish are going to be most active. Try to concen-

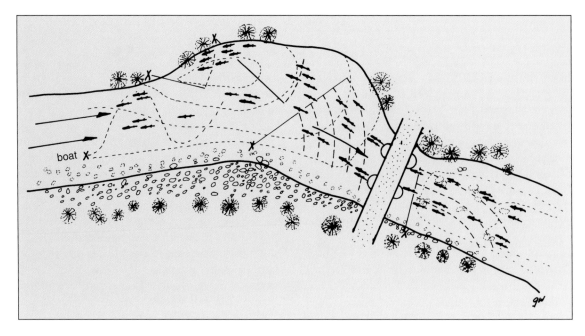

Covering normal spring flows. (X marks your position.)

trate your efforts around dusk, or dawn or on cloudy overcast days. For these times I'd go with drifting or sweeping a medium-size spoon. Since fish will be active throughout the water column, I'd alternate between working it deep, high and jigging it. You can also move it a little faster than you would in heavier water. As for spoon finish, I'd opt for something dull with good, strong contrasts.

Clear, daylight fishing is also worth a shot if you make some adjustments. Drifting and sweeping to a grid pattern is still the best way to cover the water, but for cool-water daylight conditions, spoons with brighter, flashier finishes will attract more fish. My first choice would be something in silver (or pearl) and blue.

NIGHT FISHING

The water still isn't clear enough to make night fishing a good bet, but if you want to try anyway you can approach it pretty much the same as you would on heavier water – using big dark spoons, big noisy spinners, and big dark wake-

A three-pound (1.5kg) May fish field-dressed and ready for the oven.

Tip: Stay with a Shoal

Hunting fish tend to move in small groups or shoals. If you've taken one, there is a good chance of taking another from the same spot. So don't move on too soon.

---

lures. Sweeping them high, even on the surface, will give you the best chances for a take.

HARLING

Harling can be extremely effective in late spring when fish are spread out and more active. A boat lets you cover a lot of water quickly and thoroughly, and you've got the option of fishing more than one rod. Upstream trolling (harling) with ledgered plugs combined with back-trolling spoons, or ledgered plugs or flutter-spoons, can prove deadly, especially when the fish are feeding.

Summer River Tactics

By the onset of summer, most rivers have dropped back to normal levels or even lower. The water has warmed to over 56°F (13°C) and cleared-up to six or more feet (2m) of visibility. On some flows, features like pools, runs and glides have become clearly distinguishable again.

On the rivers I fish, summer fishing is called hard fishing. There is good reason. First, over-wintered kelts and other fish that were there in the spring actively feeding have all returned to summer ranges in the salt. The targets now are very different fish, mainly early running spawners. Many of these will have little interest in feeding or in striking a lure. On top of that, because the water is warmer than sea trout like it and usually low and clear, these fish will be very edgy and much more easily spooked than at other times of the year. Hopeless? Not completely, but success on summer rivers takes careful planning. The key is learning how to

target specific pieces of water, where fish hold at specific times of the day and night.

Fishing Summer Floods

First, as I said, some rivers continue to flood on a cyclical basis right on through the summer. If you are on one of those, then your best approach is to fish the higher water just like you do in the spring. Your best chances will come with the early stages of rising water and as the water begins to drop and clear again. Target the semi-opaque, 'lager beer/weak coffee' conditions at dusk and dawn. You can use the same lures and presentations as you did in the spring.

Fishing the up and down sides of summer floods will also increase your chances of covering taking fish. Spawners usually run in from the sea on high water. These fresh-runs are much more likely to take a lure than stale fish are, i.e. those that have been in the river longer. What about clear low-water summer conditions? What's the best way to approach them?

First, once the river has dropped and cleared to summer lows, you won't find sea trout spread out through the water like they were in late spring. So casting to a grid isn't the best way to cover them. Instead, you'll want to target specific holds. Where these are will depend mainly on light levels.

Fishing Clear, Low, Summer Water in Daylight

In full summer daylight larger sea trout will tend to hold in the deeper, slower currents of pools and glides, or in the shadows of boulders or other structures like bridge pilings, even under shaded banks, roots and overhanging vegetation. Other fish, mainly finnock, will often sit in the faster, broken water of runs or the heads of pools.

Because they are skittish and warm, summer fish will not be easily taken. One tactic is to try covering the deeper fish by drifting a very small dull-pattern spoon through their holds. They are easily spooked so it's best to make your cast from below the target water or throw a long line from well above. Keep quiet and keep low! Wade out deeply or stay back from the water's edge.

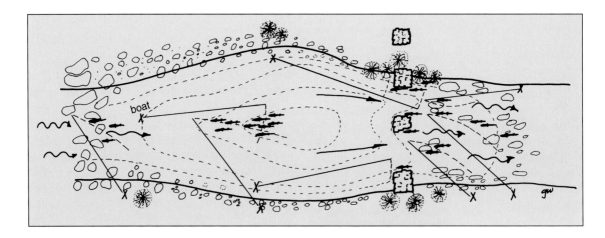

ABOVE: Covering clear low summer water in daylight. (X marks your position.)

LEFT: Runs like this are prime daylight targets under low-water summer conditions.

Fishing the faster water is probably a better bet. Try upstreaming a small dull spinner or spoon.

You can increase your chances by fishing these daytime holds when it's very cloudy or overcast – even better, at dusk. A light drizzle that breaks otherwise calm surfaces of pools and glides can also help. Edgy summer sea trout feel more secure under these conditions and will be more willing to take.

Fishing Clear, Low, Summer Water at Night
Your chances of taking summer fish improve drastically once the sun goes down. When water is clear and low, sea trout feel most secure under the cloak of darkness, from dusk until dawn. That's when they are most active and that's when they are most willing to take a lure. In the British Isles, summer fishing is nearly synonymous with night fishing and that's when most sea trout are taken. Fishing in darkness isn't to everybody's taste but under low-water summer conditions it's really the only tactic with good odds for success.

To be most effective at night you need to target different holding water, even different fish, than you did during the day. Sea trout usually run upriver at night. Favourite places to rest after pushing through faster water are the shallow tails of pools or smooth glides. These resting fish, which can be fresh from the sea, are known to be very takeable.

So your primary night target should be pool and glide tails, but don't bungle it! It's just as easy to spook fish in clear, low water at night, especially when the moon is out. So use stealth: tread softly, stay low, wade deeply or not at all, and watch your shadow. Night-fishing experts like Falkus suggest avoiding fishing these pools and glides altogether until it is good-and-dark.

The standard presentation for spin as well as fly-anglers is to sweep a lure across the pool, tail high in the water with good speed. A smaller swimming spoon is perfect for the job. Colour is irrelevant because the fish will only see contrasts. Many recommend a dark lure because it throws a good silhouette: a gold and black zebra pattern is a favourite. If it is a very dark night you might also try surface-sweeping a

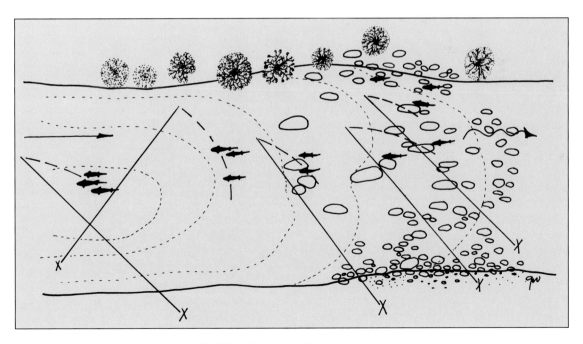

Covering clear low summer water at night. (X marks your position.)

Little pools like this are best left until nightfall.

big wake plug. Some fish will still be occupying their daylight holds, so these can also be targeted; and don't overlook the shallow riffles for any actively feeding fish.

As long as the night stays warm, then high, fast presentations can be used effectively right through until sun-up. If the night turns cold, which is pretty common toward the end of summer, then you'll want to try slower deeper presentations instead. Sea trout are very sensitive to sudden temperature changes. Cold air on warm water is a shock. Fish tend to become inactive and sit in a temporary stupor in deeper holds until they can adjust to the change. This is what sea-trouters mean when they say the fish have 'gone down'. A rapid drop in the barometer can have the same effect. Fish that have 'gone down' aren't going to be easy to take. Your best bet is to go for them like you would cold-water fish – with a big lure fished deep and slow. Any swimming spoon with good contrasts will do. I'd use my pearl, blue and black Salmo all-rounder.

Summer Clear, Low-Water Harling

Harling in low summer water is usually restricted to working the deeper pools and glides. A couple of approaches can be effective. One is to anchor the boat at the head of a big pool or glide and use it as a platform for making the same presentations (drifting and sweeping) as you would on foot. It can also give you a way to cover deep-holding fish by backing-down a small drift spoon. On really long pools or glides, back-trolling (harling) a small lure can also be an effective move.

If you are going to work a clear pool or shallow glide with a boat, don't disturb it by trolling (harling) up through it first like you might on higher spring rivers. If you need to go upstream to get yourself into position, try to move along the edge instead of over the target water. If you can't avoid running through it, let the fish settle back down for an hour or so before you start fishing. I kill the time by trolling (harling) further up-stream.

Autumn River Tactics

Autumn means cooler conditions: water temperatures dropping back into the ideal zone between 47 and 56°F (8–13°C), and even cooler air, especially at night. Generally speaking this means better fishing than during the summer. For one thing cool fish are more willing to take a lure than warm fish. For another, this is when many rivers get their main or 'harvest' runs of fish, so there are a lot more targets around.

How best to score with autumn sea trout will depend to a large degree on water level. If it is a wet autumn, then you can fish the high water just like you would in the spring. If it's dry, then you'll need to approach low-water conditions a little differently than you did in the summer, to be effective.

Autumn Normal-to-Low-Water Tactics

Targeting the best autumn holds shouldn't be a problem. Autumn fish occupy pretty much the same normal-to-low-water holds as summer fish do. You can fish them pretty much the same way too, only now you'll want to go to a slightly bigger lure and to fish it with greater variation in speed, depth and action. Deep drifting, drift-jigging, high sweeping, low sweeping, jig-sweeping and upstreaming should all be tried.

Your best chances of finding takers will be at dusk, and on cloudy, overcast days. Because autumn fish aren't as edgy as summer fish,

trying them in broad daylight can also pay. Night fishing can still be effective too, but you'll want to pay close attention to temperature. If the air is much colder than the water, fish will have 'gone down' and you'll need to go after them with lures fished deep and slow just like on a cold summer night.

For harling the same tactics apply as during summer.

This ten-pounder nailed a high-sweeping spoon on a warm June night.

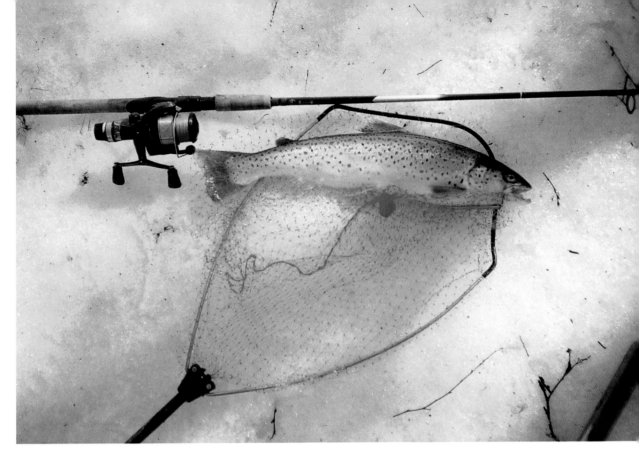

This two-pound over-wintering fish nailed a deep-sweeping Salmo All-rounder.

Winter River Tactics

There are mild winters and there are hard winters. You might not think it but mild winters make poor river-fishing. If water temperature never drops much below 40–45°F (4 to 7°C), few fish will stay in the river after they've spawned, so few will be around to catch. That means your mild-winter targets will be limited to late-running spawners and kelts on their way out to sea. A mild winter also means a wet winter and cycles of high-coloured water. If these are the winter conditions you are dealing with, the best way to make the most of them is to fish them just like you would in the spring or during a wet autumn: same lures, same presentations, same times. Unfortunately, there is a

good chance that any fish you do catch will be in poor to very poor condition and you'll probably want to return it.

Hard winters are better. Not only will more kelts stay around until spring, but all those shiny fish that have been eating themselves fat in the sea and estuaries will move up into the river to

OPPOSITE: A back-trolled spoon found this seven-and-a-half pounder lying in a deep pool at mid-day.

Tip: Try Challenging Spawners

If you are near the spawning grounds in late autumn and normal tactics aren't working, you might be able to get a strike out of male spawners by challenging them. Try deep-sweeping a big strong-pattern spoon and see what happens.[55]

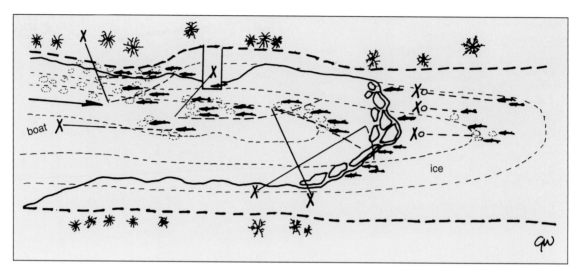

Covering winter currents. (X marks your position).

over-winter (and feed) out of the salt. Some of these will be large, mature sea trout but the majority will be younger fish, probably right around legal taking size. In Denmark they call them greenlanders because they resemble Greenland char. Now you're in business. If you don't mind fishing in the cold and learning the right tactics, a hard winter can be a real bonanza!

First thing you need to do is find winter holds. Pools and glides 6–12ft (2–3.5m) deep with a stable flow and large gravel and boulder bottoms are ideal.[56] There are usually more of these in the lower reaches of the river, so concentrate your efforts there if possible. Otherwise, undercut banks, vegetation or woody debris, around built structures, deeper turbulent water, under shelves of ice that form along the banks or in calmer stretches of water are all potential winter holds. Don't overlook the downstream side of groundwater inlets or springs but remember, with their slowed winter metabolism ice-water sea trout have a harder time navigating falls, fish ladders or even strong rapids, so stay on the sea-side of these when possible.[57]

Now, how to take over-wintering sea trout? First, these aren't spawning fish so they will keep feeding right through the winter. Only, due to slowed metabolism, not nearly as frequently – maybe only every couple of days.[58] Drift-feeding near the bottom will be the mode, with the bigger fish feeding mainly at dusk and the smaller ones more opportunistically.

As for tactics, it's imperative to remember that ice-water sea trout have slowed reaction times and lower swimming speeds. So whatever you use its got to be visible enough to attract attention and elicit a strike, and slow enough to be caught easily.

Very cold winter flows are usually also very clear, so if you are working pieces of open, unfrozen water, deep drifting can be a very effective move. A medium to large size driftspoon with strong-pattern is a good choice. Some anglers use the same colour patterns they use for turbid water. I have good luck with simple pearl and blue or pearl and black patterns or with my Salmo all-rounder. Very slow, deep sweeping can also be effective. Swimming spoons, big spinners, even ledgered plugs will work. For fishing the deeper pockets in heavier glides (favoured holding water for bigger fish), try roll-ledgering a flutter-spoon.

Winter Harling

You can also try covering winter holds from a harling boat – either by anchoring above the target water and casting to it, or by trolling (harling) through it. Remember to keep the leader fairly short – no more than 2 or 3ft (60–100cm) if you are fishing a flutter-spoon. Otherwise you'll be fishing too high off the bottom.

If the water is frozen, you'll need to make some adjustments. Partially frozen rivers can actually be a bonus. Ice-shelves that form along the bank are excellent positions to cast from. Don't forget, smaller sea trout often hold beneath ledges or patches of river ice. Work the near-bank ice-margin by backing-down, hanging and slow stop-and-go retrieves with a big spoon or spinner. If there is a lot of floating ice you can try drifting a heavy spoon with it, or sweeping under it (*see* Dealing with Drift Ice in Chapter 3).

Ice-Fishing

If your river is nearly or completely frozen over, ice-fishing can be very effective. Try to position your holes over known winter-lies. Hopefully you'll have already noticed these during the warmer seasons; or ask experienced icers, or use a grid. Backing-down, hanging and slow stop-and-go retrieves with the same lures you use on ice-free water should do the trick (*see* Fishing Currents Through the Ice in Chapter 3).

Due to slowed metabolism, ice-water sea trout probably aren't as easily spooked as they are during other seasons, even when the water is clear and low. Still, play it safe and use stealth, especially if you can actually see the fish. Finally, if winter comes on fast, fish may go-down for a time and be very hard to coax into taking a lure. Give them a few weeks to adjust to the ice-water conditions and things should pick up.[59]

Tactics for Tailwaters

Some anglers avoid tailwaters for aesthetic reasons. Fair enough, but if you are avoiding

---

> **Tip: When Losing Ice-Water Fish**
>
> If you are losing a lot of fish you are hooking, and the water is very cold, chances are they are having a hard time catching your lure cleanly. You can try slowing your presentations down further, or using a lure with less action like a spinner, coast wobbler or ledgered Devon. Or you can try drifting the smallest spoon you can manage.

---

them because you think that a power-dam ruins your chances of taking sea trout, think again. Tailwaters can offer just as good fishing as other rivers. Under some conditions even better. So, if you don't mind the looks of a tailwater, you might want to give it a spin!

Actually, tailwaters have a lot in common with rivers. Both cycle between high- and low-water conditions and both can be fished effectively in pretty much the same ways (*see* Tactics for Rivers above). One big difference is that tailwaters change a lot more frequently than rivers do because the flow is tied more closely to dam discharges than to rainfall or snow melt. As far as tactics go, this is a mixed blessing. On the one hand, because of the constant fluctuations in water level, tailwater sea-trout spend a lot less time in established lies and a lot more time moving around. This makes it harder to target specific holding water, so grid tactics are usually more efficient. On the up-side, tailwaters rarely run dead clear, so you get more opportunities to fish ideal 'lager beer/weak coffee' conditions.

Tailwaters are also more predictable. Water-releases normally happen on a set schedule. You can learn that schedule and use it to tactical advantage. For example, on the tailwaters I fish, water-releases are tied to power consumption. You can pretty much count on the water rising every work-day morning and then dropping again every evening. On weekends, it's usually lower with smaller fluctuations.

Tailwaters are prime places to find sea trout during hard winters.

As on other rivers, the best fishing comes on the up and down sides of peak flows. On tailwaters you know when this will happen, so you can be there to make the most of it. As elsewhere, fishing is usually at its best when these times coincide with dawn or dusk, or when the day is cloudy or overcast.

You can cover most all the situations you will run into on tailwaters using the same tactics you would for similar conditions on other rivers. You can fish them on foot, wading or from a boat. As always, the key to success is keeping a close eye on changing conditions and making the right adjustments.

A word of caution: water-level changes can happen very fast on a tailwater, so be careful if you are wading or in a boat or working from the ice. There are also a couple of situations unique to tailwaters that you need to look for. These occur when the conditions become extreme – either when it is very cold or very warm.

Hard-Winter Tactics for Tailwaters
The water below power-dams is usually a little warmer than normal during cold weather.[60] This makes tailwaters prime refuges for sea trout escaping the salt during hard winters. The same tactics you use on ice-water river fish will work here too, with some slight adjustments.

First, as I noted above, because there are fewer stable winter lies to target, grid-casting is the best way to cover the water efficiently. Second, because warmer fish take more readily than colder fish, you can maximize your chances by targeting warmer stretches of water. Where these are will depend on light levels and air temperature. During low-light periods, like dawn to dusk, and cloudy, overcast or snowy days when the air is much colder than the water, the warmest water will be closest to the dam outflow. On a sunny day, especially if the air warms above water temperature like it often does in late winter, then the warmest water will tend to be further downstream. Where I fish, the typical late-winter routine is to start up near the dam outflow in the morning and work down-current to the pack-ice by mid-afternoon.

Ice-fishing is also an option. You can use the same tactics you would on frozen rivers but be extra careful, since unexpected discharges can crack or break up ice.

Hot-Summer Tactics for Tailwaters

Very hot summers are also special situations for tailwaters. Because tailwaters are usually cooler than normal summer water, they provide good temporary holds for spawning fish. Again, you can fish them effectively with

This broad-gauge tailwater-brownie was a welcome surprise to my deep-sweeping Salmo All-rounder.

standard summer tactics, if you make some adjustments.

During a warm, sunny day, when the air is much warmer than the water, the coolest water – and therefore your most strike-willing fish – will be found close up to the dam outflow, sometimes right at the base of the dam. So this is where you'll want to be on a hot, sunny day, but check the regulations first. A lot of tailwaters have a minimum fishing distance of a couple of hundred yards (metres) or so. Still, get as close as you are allowed.

Once the light dies down, and especially if the air cools to below water temperature as it often does on a late-summer's night, then the cooler pieces of water – and the most takeable fish – will be found further downstream. If you want to make the most of low-light periods, then that's the water you should be targeting.

Tactics for Estuaries

An estuary is any body of brackish water that connects a river to the sea but they can go by a whole range of local names, depending on where you are, including bay, inlet, fjord, lagoon, loch, voe, stome, sea pool, tidal marsh, lough and others. To make things more confusing, many waters that are neither brackish nor connected to a river can have these same names. For tactical purposes, those are best approached as salt-water coastlines or freshwater lakes (discussed below). Brackish estuaries are different. Sea trout use them differently than other waters and so they require different tactics.

Basic Approach to Estuaries

Estuaries can be complicated places to fish. This is especially true for big, tidal bodies, where the shoreline is irregular and the water level is nearly always changing. However, there are a couple of things you can do right up front to make things easier.

Bathymetric Maps
The first, is to get hold of a good, detailed

bathymetric map. This is essentially a map of the bottom of the estuary showing depths of the contours or isobaths. Try to get one with narrow elevation intervals of a few feet (1m) or less. By reading the contours you'll be able to see where the main water channels run and where the deeper pools are, even when high water makes it nearly impossible to see them from the surface. This is important because sea trout actually use very little of an estuary, and it's along the main channels and pools that they mainly travel and hold. If you've got a boat with a sonar fish finder – even better if it's tied to a GPS navigation system – you can take your own readings and make your own maps.

Tide Tables
If your estuary also experiences tides, then the second thing you'll want to get before you start is a good tide table. This will let you anticipate changes in water level, current force and direction, so you can target the best times and conditions. As you'll see from the tables, there are usually two tide cycles every 24 hours, two high-tides and two low-tides. The difference between high- and low-tide water-marks also changes over a lunar month (around 28 days): the greatest differences occur during full and dark (new) moons and are called spring tides. The least variation occurs during the two quarter-moon phases and are called neap tides.

Choosing Estuaries
Once you know the lay of the bottom and the tidal cycles, figuring the best way to fish any estuary will depend partly on how it is built and partly on which season you fish it. There are long, narrow, sandy, tidal estuaries that you fish a lot like a river or tailwater. Big, sandy, non-tidal estuaries that you fish more like a lake or the sea. And a whole range in between. Which hold sea trout, and in which seasons, and if and how they will take a lure, are usually pretty hard to predict. This is where local information can be invaluable. In general, estuaries with variagated bottoms of mixed sand and gravel, patches of dark mud and weed beds, and where

A good bathymetric map can help you find the best target water.

there is a clearly defined channel with well-developed resting and holding pools, is your best bet. Even better if it has tides so you can predict likely taking conditions and adjust your tactics accordingly. Otherwise, you will need to keep a closer eye on wind direction, river currents and water temperature to judge where fish are going to be and when.

Choosing Season

As for choosing which seasons to fish, it's important to remember that most estuaries hold few sea trout most of the year. It's better to think of them as temporary holding waters. Estuaries can serve as portals for fish on their way into fresh water to spawn. They can serve as brackish water refuges for sea trout escaping the salt during the colder months. These are often the same estuaries but not always. Some non-migratory estuaries also hold over-wintering sea trout. Some will over-winter fish from other river systems.

One way to account for all this complexity is to think about estuary tactics as targeting essentially two different kinds of fish during two different seasons.

Late-Spring to Early-Fall Tactics for Estuaries

Most estuary sea-trouting is done during the warmer months from late-spring to early-fall. It's aimed at taking migrating fish. In some estuaries, anglers do very well, in others not. Part of the difference is probably due to the composition of the runs. Experts like Hugh Falkus once suggested that sea trout from some rivers have a natural tendency to stop feeding once they enter brackish water, while fish from others continue to feed (and take lures). The age-composition of the runs is probably also a factor. Estuaries that get a higher percentage of finnock usually fish better, simply because these younger fish take easier than older spawning fish, once they've left the salt. The locals will

Fishing falling estuary water (X marks your position.)

know which estuaries fish better in warm weather.

Fishing Falling Estuary Water

In tidal estuaries, the standard tactic is to fish the water the same way you do a spate river or tailwater. This means you focus your efforts on the falling, clearing water of a receding tide. The routine is to fish in and around the main channel. Since water will be high and a little coloured, sea trout will be spread up and down the channel, including fresh fish that have just run in on the rising tide. Any feeding fish will be foraging through weed beds in the shallower margins.

ON FOOT

If you are working on foot, a good way to cover the water is casting to a grid or fan-casting. Since the water won't be too cold, sweeping a swimming spoon or spinner – high, low and jig-sweeping – can all be very effective. If the water is still pretty turbid, try something with a strong pattern. Keep the speed down and the spacing between casts close.

As the water drops further and reaches ideal 'lager beer/weak coffee' clarity, features of the main channel will begin to emerge. You can now wade out toward them and begin targeting the pool tails and glides. Also take special care covering water on the down-current side of any reefs, rock features, little points or other structures like bridges, pilings, weirs and so on. These are favourite places for fish drift-feeding on food washed loose by the tide, so drifting a spoon or spinner through them can pay off. If it's sunny, go with something flashy; if cloudy, something dull. Silver (or pearl) and blue are well-known combinations for taking newly arrived estuary trout.

As the tide reaches low or ebb levels, and the water slows and clears further, fish will drop into the deeper channels and pools and become more difficult to take – at least during the day. So, many anglers leave the low water for night-time and fish it the same way they would a river in low summer water (*see* Fishing Clear Low Summer Water at Night above).

If you are fishing in daylight, try instead to move down with the current so you hit each pool in turn at the later stages of the ebb but before the water clears and drops to dead low. It's called 'fishing the tide down' and it can be a very efficient tactic, where the main channel is known and accessible on foot. You can also cover water quickly since you don't need to change lures. Some anglers even dispense with fishing the early stages of the ebb altogether and concentrate solely on covering each successive stretch as conditions reach ideal.

FROM A BOAT

Another option is to fish from a drifting boat. This is clearly the best way to fish in estuaries, where following the receding tide on foot across soft ground can be difficult, if not down right dangerous when there is quicksand to worry about. Both casting and back-trolling (harling) can be very effective.

Fishing Rising Estuary Water

Many estuary anglers avoid fishing the rising water – finding it a better use of time to fish the falling tide. This doesn't mean fish won't take in rising water. Harris and Morgan note the mysterious tendency of fish in some pools to go-on-the-feed just before the water begins to rise. In my experience, this is also true for rivers and tailwaters. Maybe the fish anticipate the improved hunting conditions with rising water, maybe it's a reaction to slight pressure changes at the turn-of-the-tide. Either way, it's worth having a small spoon or spinner in the water when it happens.

How about fishing the rising water right through? Sure, this can also be a good move, especially when it's very warm, say 60°F (15°C) and higher. Rising tides, especially spring tides, bring in cooler water from the sea. Sea trout holding in deeper, cooler water near the estuary mouth will sometimes follow these cooler currents up the estuary to hunt, only to drop back out as the tide recedes. Fishing a stretch of channel right through its cycle of rising and

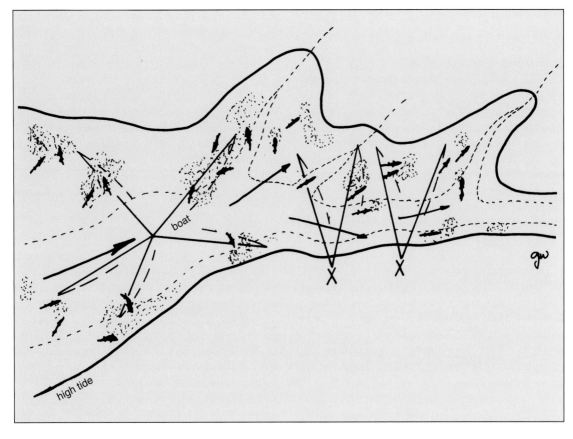

Fishing rising estuary water (X marks your position.)

falling water will increase your odds of making contact with them.

If you are on foot, an effective tactic can be to fish up the main channel along with the rising water. Try, if you can, to move up with the tide as the water reaches ideal clarity. Since these fish will be foraging mainly in shallower weed beds on the margins of the main channel, concentrate on covering these. Sweeping a spoon high in the water to stay above the weeds can be very effective. However, it is often much easier to pull this ploy off from a boat (light trolling). If the current is strong enough you can slowly drift up the main channel while making casts into the shallower margins. You can also troll a lure using a side-planer.

Fishing the Estuary Mouth

Another way to respond to very warm conditions is to fish the deeper, cooler water near the estuary mouth. It's sometimes possible to cover this on foot if you can find some point close enough to the deeper channels to cast from. Bridges, piers, promontories, jetties, reefs, sea walls, docks can all be valuable bases to work from.

It is often more efficient to cover these deep holds from a boat, especially if it is rigged up with a sonar fish-finder. Fish may be holding anywhere up to 50ft (15.5m) but drop-offs on either side of the main channel are usually the most productive. Deep jigging a spoon from a drifting or anchored boat can be very effective.

ABOVE: Bridges are great bases to cover deeper estuary channels from when you're fishing on foot. BELOW: Fishing the estuary mouth (X marks your position.)

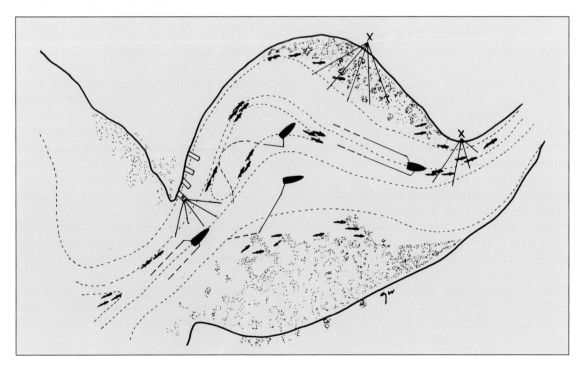

So can deep-trolling a spoon or plug. As always, adjust lure finish to water clarity and lighting. Remember that deeper water is also darker, so think about going with colours that show best in low light, like blues, chartreuse, fluorescents, white and glo-paint finishes.

Fishing Non-Tidal Estuaries

Fishing an estuary where there is little or no tide is similar to fishing tidal flows, with a few important differences. First, you still want to target features along the main channel like drop-offs, pools, glides, structures and shallow weed beds. But, instead of keeping an eye on the tide-tables to determine best times and tactics, it's river flow, wind direction and water temperature that will dictate your best moves.

As elsewhere, fishing the water when it's falling and clearing is usually the most efficient daylight tactic, while night fishing is the best way to approach low summer water. In some estuaries you may need to wait until after the spring floods to find good daylight conditions, and even later into summer to find water clear enough to make night fishing worthwhile.

Without the cooling effects of high-tides non-tidal estuary water can get very warm by late-summer. This often happens when winds blow warmer surface waters up the estuary. When this happens, it's best to shift your activities toward the cooler, deeper water near the estuary mouth. On the other hand, a good sustained down estuary wind will push warmer surface water out and drag cooler deeper water up the estuary, and sea trout will follow.

Late-Fall to Early-Spring Tactics for Estuaries

How an estuary fishes during the colder months often depends on just how cold it gets. Recall that sea trout have a problem dealing with cold salt-water – the colder the water, the less they can tolerate it. So whether or not fish actually enter an estuary during the winter, and where to find them if they do, is mainly a matter of water temperature. Generally speaking, the colder the water, the further up the estuary sea trout will

penetrate. So the best policy is to target lower sections at the beginning of the season, or during mild winters, and move higher up as the season progresses and the water cools.

Mild-Winter Estuary Tactics

If the winter is very mild and sea-water never gets much below 50°F (10°C), few fish will enter brackish water and fishing will be poor. If it gets colder, many will move in to over-winter, and fishing can be good right into spring. Several kinds of fish will be available: repairing kelts, younger greenlanders and older sea-trout that did not spawn that year.

When the water temperature is between 40 and 47°F (4–8°C) estuary fishing is at its best. Trout will be fairly active, feed occasionally and be ready takers. Try targeting the same places you do in warmer weather and use the same tactics. You can fish the tides the same too. Only now you'll want to bump lure-size up and speed down a notch and to keep your presentations deep.

In the colder, more oxygen-rich water, winter fish will visit the stiller shallows to hunt, so target these also. Shallow waters over a dark muddy bottom often fish well after the sun has warmed them up. These are perfect places to cover with a coast wobbler or wide-bodied spoon cast from shore or from a drifting boat further out. You can also try trolling (light trolling) a spoon or plug off a long unweighted line, maybe with a side-planer to cover the near-shore flats.

Keep a close eye on wind direction too, especially if you are in non-tidal waters. A breeze that blows warmer surface water up the estuary can trigger activity and bring on the bite.

Hard-Winter Estuary Tactics

Estuaries can also fish well during harder winters, but sea trout change behaviour as water nears freezing, so you'll need to adjust your tactics. First, you'll probably want to relocate. Once water drops below 40°F (4°C) fish will often move up to the head of the estuary or near the outlets of feeder streams to find even fresher water. Sea-trout metabolism and reaction speed slow way down when it gets really cold. Remember, cold fish are much less active and only feed every couple of days or so. This doesn't mean they can't be taken. You might find them holding in the same places you found migrating fish during the warmer months. Look for the deeper holes and glides, where water flow and height are more or less steady. These are prime places for taking bigger fish early and late in the day when they are most active. Don't overlook the sun-warmed shallows either for shoals of smaller hunting fish.

As for presentations – slow and low is always the best ice-water formula. Drifting, sweeping, hanging and stop-and-go with big strong-pattern lures are good bets. If you've got a boat, you can use it to position yourself ideally for slow, deep presentations. Trolling (light trolling) can also be effective but you'll want to keep to a crawl. As always, watch the wind. If you are fishing in water with little or no tidal effect, winds can make all the difference. Don't forget the funny effects of near-freezing water: once it chills to under 40°F (4°C), it gets lighter, so you'll be looking for a breeze that blows down the estuary. This will push the colder water out and drag warmer deeper water in, and improve your chances of scoring.

What if the estuary freezes over? No problem. If it's only partially frozen you can fish from the edge of the ice – but be really careful! If it's frozen solid right over, you can still target the same ice-water holds using ice-fishing tactics (*see* Fishing Currents Through the Ice and Fishing Through the Ice in Still Waters in Chapter 3).

If you find yourself following fish further up into freshwater, then go with your normal ice-water tactics for rivers or tailwaters (*see* Winter River Tactics and Hard-Winter Tactics for Tailwaters above).

Tactics for Coastlines

There are three basic keys to taking sea trout in coastal waters.[61] I'll start with inshore or near-shore fishing first, what some anglers call fishing the 'skinny water'.

Near-Shore Tactics

The first key is to find the right stretch of beachfront. A wrong choice here and you can end up wasting a lot of time. Walk out on to an open shoreline and you'll see why. Where do you start? Talk about intimidating. It makes fishing rivers, and even estuaries, seem like shooting fish in a barrel by comparison. However, it isn't all good holding water and it's not too difficult to narrow it down to what is.

Locating Near-Shore Holding Water
First, bear in mind that in coastal waters we are dealing with actively feeding fish. After all, that's why sea trout take to the salt – to eat and get fat. Find their prey and you've found them. Rocky or stony and irregular coastlines with inlets, bays and jutting-out reefs are where to start. You want to look for stretches of shoreline where the bottom is mixed patches of sand, rock and seaweed – what's called a 'leopard bottom' in the southern Baltic. This is where you'll find the small crustaceans, shrimps, fry, sand worms and bait fish that sea trout hunt in the salt. Even better if you can see deeper water not too far out, where sea trout can take refuge in low water or when it gets hot. Now if this piece of likely looking beachfront is also adjacent to a known spawning route, like a river mouth or estuary, then you are probably in business – but that's no guarantee, so it's a good idea to check with the locals before getting your line wet.

Fishing Near-Shore Currents
Once you've nailed down a piece of coastal holding water, the next key to success is learning how to read and fish the coastal currents. Almost all coastal waters have currents. In tidal waters these are pretty clear and follow regular lunar cycles. In waters where tidal fluctuations are negligible, like in the Baltic, water currents can be less regular and local conditions like wind play a bigger role. On both kinds of

Stretches of shoreline like this are usually worth a shot, especially if near a known sea trout river.

coastlines, sea trout use the currents to hunt for prey. Basically they follow the flow, and basically so should the spin-angler.

First, when sea trout are not actively feeding they tend to hold further out from the shoreline in somewhat deeper water (6–12ft or 2–3.5m) close to cover – usually under and around the edges of weed beds and rocky features. To cover them, the normal tactic is to wade out or take up position on a stony reef or point and make a series of round-the-clock casts. Here is where a longer rod of, say, 10ft (3m), loaded with thin braid, is an advantage. Snagging weeds is a constant problem but it can't be helped if you want to cover these fish from shore. An effective alternative can be covering them from a light boat anchored just beyond the weed beds in deeper water.

When feeding actively, sea trout usually move in very close to shore. In tidal waters this is often triggered by a rising tide (flood tide). It can also be triggered by an on-shore wind. As the water moves in and, most commonly, diagonally along the beach, sea trout follow the current in to forage for food that the waves have kicked up and to hunt the smaller fish that are doing the same.

A good tactic now is to walk along with the current while making a series of parallel casts more or less perpendicular to the shore to cover the hunting fish. Even in clear water it's probably a good idea to space your casts no more than 6ft (2m) apart – the maximum size of the sea trout's strike zone. As elsewhere, it's also a good idea to cover the nearest shallow water with a cast or two before wading in.

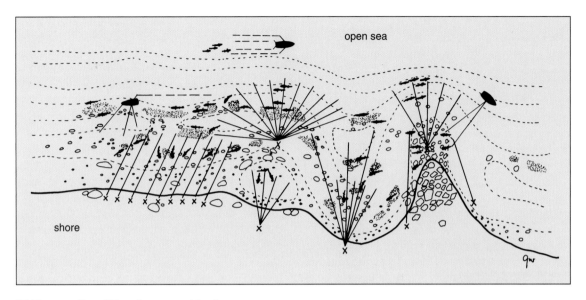

Fishing coastlines (X marks your position.)

You can also cover these near-shore fish from a drifting dinghy by either casting or light trolling.

Feeding fish are especially attracted to near-shore features like underwater reefs, shell banks, rocky points and boulders. So these should be targeted too. Where the current is strong enough, especially on the ebb tide, fish will sometimes position themselves on the down-current side of these features to drift-feed on foods that have been washed loose. So, a good move is to work the water on the down-current side thoroughly: if the current moves to the right, cover the water on the right side; if it goes left, cover the water on the left. Again you can hit these targets on foot or in a light boat from further out.

The best lures and presentations to use will depend on seasonal conditions, which I'll discuss below. Light to medium weight ($^{1}/_{4}$–$^{2}/_{3}$oz or 7–18g) swimming spoons, spinners (#1 to #3) and semi-buoyant coast wobblers will cover most situations fishing from shore. For light trolling, Toby-like casting spoons, flutter-spoons and crankbaits are the most popular. As far as choosing the best lure finish, the most effective coast lures tend to be more subdued than those used in rivers because the water is generally clearer. Otherwise the same principles apply. Jan Johansson, author of *Havsöringsfiske*, makes the following recommendations: for clear water, cloudy weather – silver, copper and gold combination patterns; for clear water, sunny conditions – silver with green back; for coloured water – copper with dark markings; and for night fishing – black or gold and black zebra patterns.

Responding to Near-Shore Water Temperature

The third key to doing well on beachfronts is working the effects of water temperature into your tactics. As we have seen, sea trout have a problem adjusting to salt-water when it is very cold. So when these coastal waters chill down to under 47°F (8°C) most sea trout move into brackish estuaries or river mouths to over-winter. So that's where you'll have better luck finding fish until things warm up a bit. If the water is anywhere between 47 and 68°F (8–20°C), the coast is always worth a shot as long as you adjust your tactics to changes in water, light and wind conditions.

Winter Near-Shore Coastal Tactics

During a mild winter or early spring, when the water is still below ideal temperature, sea trout will feed where the near-shore water is warmest. So that's where you should concentrate your efforts. Shallow water warmed by the sun will provide the best targets. Keep an eye out for depressions between the shore and first sand bar, which coasters call 'bathtubs'; also for shallow water over patches of dark bottom, and for shallow enclosed fjords and bays. All these warm up more quickly than deeper water.

Your best times to fish in winter will usually be mid-day when the shallows have had time to heat up. Wind direction will also have a big effect on how these spots fish. A wind that blows in your face (an on-shore wind) is usually best. Even though it makes casting more difficult, an on-shore wind blows sun-warmed surface water in toward the shore making it even warmer. This can trigger activity among small food organisms in the near-shore shallows, which in turn attracts feeding trout. If this also coincides with tides that peak at around mid-day, then conditions are ideal for good fishing. Off-shore winds are less good, they push the warmer water out and draw in much colder water, which can put all feeding on hold.

Claus Eriksen recommends fishing over broad stretches of water several times during the day to maximize chances of hitting shoals of feeding fish. Winter trout often hunt in groups, so seeing or taking one often means a good chance at others.

Most of the winter fish you catch will be smaller (14–17in or 36–44cm), plump and silvery greenlanders. If over the legal limit, these are close to perfect for eating. You may also come across larger thin-bodied kelts that have returned to the sea to repair from the rigors of spawning. These are less than great eating, so many anglers return them.

As for lures and presentations, remember, these are still cold-water fish with slower than normal reaction speeds. Big lures fished very slowly are the order of the day. Wider bodied swimming spoons and coast wobblers that can be retrieved very slowly, while just grazing the shallow bottom, are good choices. A slow stop-and-go presentation is often effective. Very slow-deep jigging, even bouncing or grounding the lure momentarily on the bottom, can also work.

Spring Near-Shore Coastal Tactics

With water temperatures reaching the ideal 47–56°F (8–13°C) range, coastal fish become increasingly active and much more mobile. They will often cover great distances as they hunt and forage along the beachfront. They will feed in the places they did during the winter but, with warming temperatures, also further out around weed beds, rock features, shell banks and islets. The normal tactic is to keep mobile yourself, covering as much promising water as possible in a day. Coasters call it the 'burnt petrol tactic'. It's essentially hitting four to six places a day with no more than a couple of hours at each, unless you find a shoal of takers.

Fishing can still be good during the day, especially if it's partly cloudy, but as the water warms, the best times will be when the light is lower, around dawn and dusk. Even better if these correlate with a turn-of-tide. As always, watch the wind. If the water is still fairly cold, a warming on-shore wind can help, but once temperatures reach near 60°F (15°C), on-shore winds can warm the shallows too much. Fish will avoid these in daylight. So you'll need to switch to summer tactics (see below). On the other hand, a good wind at your back can also help. It not only makes long casts easier, it can keep the shallows cooler and more fishable in daylight. Greenlanders will still make up the majority of takers, but larger sea trout in the 17–21in (44–54cm) range will be more common, and repairing kelts will already be in much better condition.

At the beginning of the season. when the water is still fairly cold, you'll want to use the same deep, slow presentations you did in winter. Once things warm up and sea trout become more active, faster more varied presentations will work best. If you are fishing on foot, try high and low sweeping, jig-sweeping and stop-and-go retrieves. You can also work from a boat. One method is to let the boat drift along the beachfront with the current while making casts in toward shore. This is an excellent way to cover lots of water searching for shoals of hunting fish. Or you can try trolling (light trolling) a light spoon or diving plug along the same stretch of coast. If the water is still not much over 47°F (8°C), using a ledger-rig will help you stay deep. Once the water warms you won't need the extra weight. Where the conditions aren't too rough, some light-trollers report success using a surface side-planer to fish lures through the near-shore shallows from further out.

Summer Near-Shore Coastal Tactics
Once the water warms to over 60°F (15°C), coastal sea trout change behaviour further. They move around a lot less, especially during daylight. Instead they hold in the deeper, cooler water further out from shore during the warmest hours, and only move into the shallows to hunt after dark. In most cases these fish are out of casting range from the beach but deep trolling can be an effective option if you've got the right gear. According to Mathias Ström of West Coast Fishing Charters on Sweden's west coast archipelago, underwater drop-offs, where the warmer, shallow water meets cooler, deeper water, should be targeted first since these are favoured holds for both sea trout and bait fish in warm weather.

The near-shore shallows are best left until the sun goes down and conditions cool. If water temperatures aren't too warm – say no higher than 68°F (20°C) – then you may find sea trout anytime from dusk till dawn hunting in the same places they did in daylight during spring. If it gets much warmer, you'll do better to target the deeper, cooler currents off reefs and points from late at night to around sunrise, when conditions are at their coolest.

Many coasters consider a tide that peeks at around midnight to be ideal, since fish will move in with the flood around dusk and back

Tip: When Fishing at Night

Danish coast angler Claus Eriksen has some tips for fishing the summer coast at night, which I've added here verbatim.

1. Do not start too early, and try resting at the end of the day. This is essential if you are going to fish in a concentrated way through the night.
2. Bring warm clothes. No matter how hot the day and the evening have been, it is cold at night. Also, as you get tired, you will feel the cold more.
3. Be prepared. Bring chocolate, and perhaps a hot drink. This can really help when you suddenly 'go cold'.
4. Remember to bring a light. A small torch for when you change bait or untangle lines, and a large torch to find your way about. Also bring some spare batteries along.
5. Be patient with sea trout. They never forage all through the night, but arrive in shoals for short periods, and so are entirely unpredictable.
6. Be sociable. In the summer there are lots of fishermen with limited room.

Seems like good advice wherever you fish at night.

out on the ebb around dawn. A wind that blows at your back is also good since it helps keep the near-shore water cooler and more fishable in hot weather.

As elsewhere, warm-water coastal trout are often reluctant takers, even at night. Very small spoons (c. ¼oz or 7g) and spinners (#1 to #3) with dark patterns fished high and fast tend to give the best results. Warm trout are also easily spooked trout, so don't forget to use stealth.

Autumn Near-Shore Coastal Tactics

Once sea-water drops back down below 60°F (15°C) coast fishing can really pick up. Sea trout will be on the move toward spawning streams and winter ranges. Greenlanders and fully repaired kelts will make up the bulk of fish. Now is also your chance to hit on much bigger sea trout returning from the open sea. All of these fish will be in prime condition.

During the early part of the season when the water is still warm your best chances will come during the early mornings and evening, but night fishing is also worth a try – all the better if you have a turning tide in your favour. Once the water cools down toward 50°F (10°C) you'll have a decent chance of taking fish almost any time from dawn to dusk unless it's calm and sunny. The best daylight fishing will be when it's cloudy, overcast and a little windy.

Since the water will be well mixed by this season, you can find sea trout anywhere along the shorefront. Concentrate on water that is moving. You may have to wade out across a couple of sand bars if the water is low or the tide out. Water off points, reefs and jetties are prime targets and these are also good positions to cast from, but don't forget to fish the bays, fjords and inlets, where there is good water circulation. Migrating fish will also run very close to the shore, especially under subdued light, so make sure you cover the shallow water before wading in. Don't forget to cover any near-shore depressions or 'bathtubs', especially during the cooler end of the season. Since fish will be moving mainly at night and holding up during the day, a good strategy is to return to prime spots every day or so. Autumn fish will often show themselves near the surface. Try covering them with something fished high and fairly fast. Since they may be moving in shoals, try to move with them if you can.

Autumn sea trout eat a lot! It's not uncommon to land fish already stuffed with food. So autumn sea trout are ready takers but, with all that food around, they can also be very picky. Many coasters advocate lighter lines or leaders (0.20–.25mm mono or 0.10–0.17mm braid),

especially when fishing in daylight. Varying your presentations between high and low, fast and slow retrieves seems to be the way to go generally. As for lures, many use the same small spoons and spinners you use during summer. Once the waters cool in later autumn, go to bigger sizes. Most autumn coasters wade but there is no reason why you can't use a boat to target the same water, just like you do in the spring (*see* Spring Near-Shore Tactics above).

Off-Shore Tactics

Now that covers the near-shore fishing. How about the fish further out? We know that in some areas, sea trout – especially larger, older fish – will head off-shore into deep water during the warmer months to hunt schools of herring, sprat and sand eels, often in company with salmon.[62] These fish are way beyond the range of the surf caster and even light trolling boat but they can be pursued effectively with more specialized deep-trolling outfits (*see* Deep Trolling in Chapter 3).

This is big sport off the East Jutland coast of Denmark. According to Steen Ulnits, the tactic is to pinpoint the location and depth of the schools and accompanying sea trout (and salmon) using sonar and GPS instruments. The fish are then covered by trolling flutter-spoons and plugs run off down-riggers and divers to depths of around 50–60ft (15.5–18.5m). Popular lures include Apex, Bomber and Abu x-Rap plugs and Northern King spoons. One of the most effective set-ups seems to be fishing a Northern King spoon behind a flasher off a Dipsy Diver. You'll need to adjust lure colour and finish to the lower light conditions deeper down. Try blue, chartreuse, black and white, fluorescents hues and glo-paint finishes.

Tip: Rinse Salt-Water Tackle

Salt-water eventually kills all tackle. To prolong its life, rinse it thoroughly in fresh water after its been in the salt.

Tactics for Lakes

Almost everything we know about taking sea trout in freshwater lakes comes from the British Isles. The reason is simple: that's where the best still water is found and the strongest traditions for fishing them. Things may change. With sea trout being introduced to more and more waters outside of Europe, the chances for taking them in lakes should increase. Until then, tactics will reflect what anglers of the British Isles have learned over many generations fishing the sea trout lochs of Scotland, Ireland and the Hebrides.

To begin with, sea trout fishing in freshwater lakes or lochs is traditionally aimed at taking migratory fish. That means fish that are using the lake as a way-station between the sea or estuary and a spawning stream. These fish may stay in the loch for anywhere from a couple of days to a couple of months, depending on the timing of the spawning runs. So the taking season tends to cover early spring to later fall on many lochs, with the best chances coming in late summer and early autumn when the main runs of fish enter.

As on other big waters, knowing what the bottom looks like is a valuable key to where the fish are. So get hold of a good detailed bathymetric map and, if you are going to be fishing from a boat, the best sonar fish finder you can afford. There are essentially two approaches to loch fishing: fishing the shallow water and fishing the deeper water

Shallow-Water Tactics for Lakes

This is the traditional approach to loch fishing. It's based on a couple of assumptions. The first is that loch trout aren't going to be the same actively feeding fish you'd find in salty coastal waters or even brackish estuaries during the winter. They will mainly be non-feeding migrators: mature sea-trout destined to spawn, and younger finnock that may or may not spawn. So, just as on the river, your main targets are going to be fresh-run fish. Remember, the longer these fish are in fresh water, the less likely they

are to feed actively. It's the fresh runs that will be the most likely takers. This is also why the best sea-trout lochs tend to be those connected to the sea by a short stretch of river or brackish bay. Lakes in the upper reaches of a system also get sea trout, but these fish will be a lot harder to catch. Jock Scott went as far as to say that success in loch fishing is 85 per cent fresh fish and 15 per cent hard work, 'if fresh fish are not in the loch, sport will be poor'.

Old-school loch-anglers approach still water about the same way they do a big pool in the river. They figure that most sea trout will be found in water no deeper than 15–20ft (4.5–6m), usually less. The main difference is scale. Since most lochs are a lot bigger than river pools, the challenge becomes locating the best shallow-water lies to cover. Knowing how the fish move and hold in a loch helps.

Locating Shallow Holding Water in Lakes
New fish that enter a loch tend to move right around the margins and then hold off the mouths of feeder streams until running time. The shallow sandy or gravelly delta banks or ridges that form off the mouths of these streams are usually first-choice targets, especially where there is deeper water just beyond. Experts like Hugh Falkus also suggest hitting the 'tail' of the lake at the outflow because fish sometimes hold there before moving further in, like they do when running up into a new river pool. Otherwise, it's common to target moving fish – some will be hunting fish – anywhere along the shallow lake margins. Little bays and inlets with rocky bottoms, submerged points, stony outcroppings and around islands are all good places. Even reed beds are worth a shot.

Reading Water, Wind and Light on Lakes
As elsewhere, reading water, wind and light conditions is basic to success in lochs. Early and late in the season, when the water is cold, presentations should be kept slow and near the bottom. Under normal conditions, dawn and dusk are generally your best taking times but

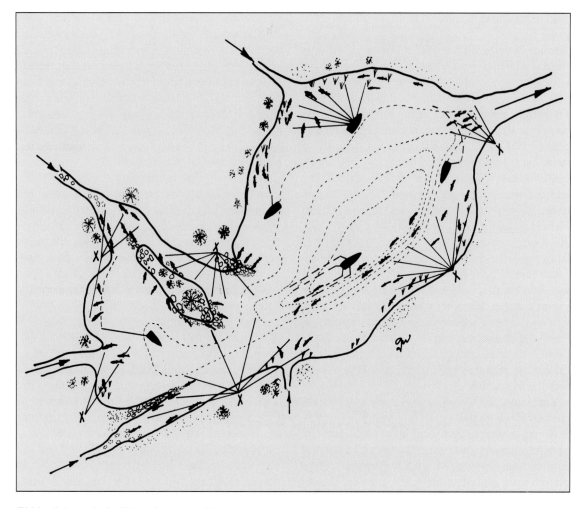

Fishing lakes or lochs (X marks your position.)

fishing sun-warmed shallows, especially with the help of a warming on-shore breeze, can also be a good cold-weather tactic. If the summer is hot and the shallows warm up too much, many fish will move out into deeper, cooler water during the daytime and only venture into the shallows after the sun has gone down. So night fishing is definitely worth the time. An off-shore breeze can also help since it brings in cooler water and sea trout with it!

As for best water height and clarity, lakes are similar to rivers and tidal waters. High flows (whether tides from below the lake or spates from above) tend to bring in fresh runs of fish, so working the falling water usually brings the best results. Lake water tends to be clearer than river currents but it can colour up near the inflows during a spate, so you'll need to adjust tactics accordingly. If it is very clear, use stealth, especially when working over still, shallow water. Most lake-fishers prefer a high, cloudy sky and choppy surface, since these help obscure their movements and reduce the likelihood of spooking fish.

The traditional way to cover shallow still-water holds is with a light boat equipped with oars and sometimes a small outboard. Fishing on foot is less common. We'll look at both,

Shallow-Water Boat Tactics for Lakes: Drifting
The most common boat tactic is drifting. One manoeuvre is to let the boat drift with the wind in toward shore as the angler covers the shallow water with round-the-clock or fan casts. Since shallow-water fish are thought to hold facing into the wind, and so also the incoming boat, a favourite variation to normal drifting is tacking. Here the boat is made to slide laterally toward the shore by using the oars, rudder or motor to tack across wind. Casts are made downwind toward land so the movement of the boat swings the lure into the fish's field of vision from a side-angle. The same presentation can be effected in still wind by rowing or motoring slowing at right angles to the shore. Once you've covered that swath of water into the shallows, the boat is rowed or powered straight out and another lateral drift begun.

Traditionally, loch-anglers tend to fish the lure higher for fresh-run sea trout early in the season and deeper as the season wears and the fish 'stale', but don't forget the effects of water temperature and clarity either. Sink-and-draw, zigzag and jigging can all be effective presentations under the right conditions.

When drifting over shallow water stealth is all important. Keep quiet, keep down, don't motor over water you intend to cover and cast a longer line than you would on the river. Many anglers also avoid fishing with the sun or moon at their back since it can dazzle the fish.

As for lure choice, the same principles apply as on other waters: bigger, strong-pattern lures for cold or coloured water; smaller, more subdued lures for warmer, clearer water. Use flashier finishes when it is bright, duller finishes when it is not (*see* Chapter 2).

Shallow-Water Boat Tactics for Lakes:
Light Trolling
Light trolling with oars or an outboard can also be effective on lochs. The usual tactic is to follow bottom contours or features where fish are known to hold. Underwater reefs, rock outcroppings, gravel bars, banks and drop-offs are favourite targets. On some lochs, teams of light boats follow traditional routes like the twenty-yard-wide (20m) taking strip along the famous Endrick bank on Loch Lomond in Scotland. Water is usually covered by manoeuvring the boat in an 'S' pattern.

Most boats fish three to five rods. Lures are trailed at different lengths so they fish anywhere from 5 to 8ft (1.5–2.5m) deep over 10–15ft (3–4.5m) of water. Ledger rigs run off 30–50yd (30–50m) of line are a common set-up but old-schoolers like Hamish Young trail much longer lines of up to 100yd (100m) to get more depth and to minimize any spook-effects of the motoring boat.

The most common light-trolling lures are Toby-type swimming spoons and crankbaits like Rapalas and Kynock Killers (called J-plugs in North America). Jock Scott also trolled floating or semi-buoyant Devons. Although not in the traditional repertory, fishing these same lures off a surface side-planer is an excellent way to cover the near-shore shallows without alarming fish.

Fishing Lakes On-Foot
If you are fishing on foot you are usually considered at a disadvantage over boaters, but that doesn't always hold. Unless the loch is shallow all over, or the fish have gone deep, most of the prime shallow-holding water can be covered on foot. Try to target times when fish are closest to shore, early and late in the day and at night. Or, if it's a cold, spring day, in the afternoon once the sun has warmed the shallows.

Try walking (or wading) along the shore while covering the water with overlapping round-the-clock casts. Some anglers opt for longer rods and thinner lines to get greater distance. Space your cast anywhere from 3 to 6ft (1–2m), depending on water clarity. Keep moving until you hit a fish, then work that spot more thoroughly for a chance at taking others out of a shoal.

Try swimming spoons, spinners or coast wobblers, sink-and-draw, zigzag and jigging. Adjust lure size and colour, and presentation speed, to water conditions; and don't forget to use stealth. If you pick the right times and places, there is no reason you have to take a back-seat to boaters!

Deep-Water Tactics for Lakes
Now that's the traditional approach to fishing lochs: sticking to the shallower water. However, in recent years, more and more loch-anglers have been taking sea trout on deep-trolling rigs. According to Hugh Falkus it all seems to have started about 30 years ago when the famous Loch Lomond angler, Harry Britton, started experimenting with a deep-trailing rig designed for lake trout (char). The contraption let you fish up to six lures off a weighted plumb-line at intervals down to about 60ft (18.5m). It must have been fantastically cumbersome to operate but both Britton and later Falkus reported taking sea trout at depths of 25–35ft (7.5–11m).

Well, the genie was out of the bag. Now most of the larger lochs have a small but growing club of deep-trolling devotees. Equipment and methods have changed, of course. Much of it has been imported or adapted from the older Great Lakes trolling tradition in the States. Basically, the tactics are the same as Danish anglers use for off-shore fish (see Off-Shore Tactics above).

On Loch Lomond, anglers use downriggers, divers and planer boards to run flutter-spoons and plugs like Rapalas and J-Plugs (Kynock Killers) down to 100ft (30m) and they report taking sea trout down to about 60ft (18.5m). Of the deep-loch trollers, James Kinnear is about the most knowledgeable I know of. He keeps a web site (www.trollscotlochs.aol.com), which is well worth checking out if you are thinking about going deep after loch fish.

Finding the Right Depth on Lakes
One of the challenges of fishing for sea trout outside the shallows has always been how deep to fish. Big lakes can be several hundred feet (100m) deep, which leaves a lot of room for error, but there are some useful rules of thumb. Generally speaking, the warmer the weather, the deeper the fish because that's where the cooler, more oxygenated layers will be – but not always. Recall that crazy law of physics that says water starts getting lighter once it cools below 40°F (4°C)? That means early and late in the season fish can also hold in deeper water because it's actually a little warmer than higher up! And to make things even more complicated, there are also periods when a lake's layers actually 'turn over', usually during spring and fall. That's when water temperature and oxygen content are mixed-up throughout the lake and fish might be found at almost any depth.

Until pretty recently water sense, a whole lot of experience and an intimate knowledge of the loch were the keys to finding deep fish. That's still important, but nowadays almost all serious loch-trollers use sonar to find and target fish (see Sonar Fish Finders and GPS in Chapter 3). The method is simple but effective. First, you reconnoitre the water until your finder registers large fish. You send your offerings down to that depth, using a downrigger, planer or diver. Then you choose a path that will run your lures through the images on the screen. These might be sea trout or they might be lake trout (char), big resident browns, pike, salmon, even a school of tightly packed bait fish, or a log. As on other waters, the best trolling speeds will depend on water temperature and, to some degree, clarity. Colder or coloured means slower; warmer or clearer means faster. From 1½–3½mph (c. 1–3kn or 0.9–1.6m/s) seems to be the most effective range. You'll also need to adjust lure colour and finish to the lower light conditions deeper down.

Over-Wintering Lake Fish?
There is still a lot to learn about taking sea trout at depth, but a few things are starting to come into focus. One is that fishing deep might let you take fish outside the normal taking period. We've always known going deep can put you in contact with fish holding outside the shallows in very warm weather, now it seems there might be

fish to take on deep-trolling gear in cold weather too. I have already mentioned Harry Britton's original success with an experimental deep-trolling rig on Loch Lomond. Seems it came very early in the season before the water had warmed up to normal taking range for traditional shallow-water methods. Today, trollers on Lomond continue to take fish deep in cold water, including kelt sea-trout down to 50ft (15.5m). Sounds like over-wintering feeding sea trout doesn't it? If so, we can add lochs to estuaries and river mouths as good winter fishing waters! Another piece of good news: deep-trollers seems to take bigger fish!

Luck, Skill and Measuring Success

Thinking tactically is essential for success with sea trout. But what about luck? One of my favourite scenes in one of my favourite films *Tombstone* is when Ike Clanton explodes in frustration after having lost a whole string of poker hands to Doc Holliday. 'What's that now?,' Clanton barks out, 'twelve hands in a row? Dammit Holliday, nobody's that lucky!' He was right, there. Gamblers like Holliday left very little to chance. Ike should have kept a closer eye on his opponent's play instead of waiting for good fortune: he might have learned a thing or two about poker.

The same goes for sea-trouting. Consistently successful anglers leave little to chance. Instead, they do all they can to get the odds in their favour. They try to fish when conditions are most favourable, and when they aren't, they make the most of them by thinking tactically and using the best moves they know in terms of lures and presentations.

That's not to say luck doesn't come into it. Sea-trout angling isn't rocket science – it's not that predictable. There is a lot we know and a lot we still don't about locating sea trout and about making them take a lure on any single day, once we have. There are simply too many variables to try to control for like weather, pressure, water level and clarity, light levels and so on. There are

also biological factors that effect individual fish differently. Some sea trout simply won't take a lure, no matter how well it's presented; others will take almost anything you toss at them. When the uncontrolled variables come together in our favour, we call it good luck; when they don't, bad luck. But fortune is random, she visits the novice as often as the expert. So, the best anybody can do is learn to read conditions and respond accordingly. Some anglers have longer experience doing that, they do it better and so they are more successful over the long run than others. That's skill, not luck.

Learning how to be more successful at sea-trouting also depends on what you mean by success. Even more basically, what you want to get out of sea-trouting. Ask any bunch of anglers why they fish and you'll probably get a whole range of answers including 'getting out in nature', 'fishing for the sheer joy of it', 'being alone', 'visiting fishing buddies' 'relaxation'. Can't argue with any of that. Who doesn't enjoy a fine day out on the water? In my experience, one of the things that divides the really successful anglers from the rest is their primary goal of catching fish. That may sound pretty obvious, but it's surprising how many anglers shy away from committing themselves to catching fish as a prime objective.

I know one casual angler who makes a point of fishing lures with dull, rusted or broken hooks. I asked him why, once. He said he didn't really care if he caught anything, which he hardly ever did! Hugh Falkus observed similar examples of what he called self-deception among some of the fishing guests he hosted. He believed many were fooling themselves to assuage disappointment. To quote the great sea-trouter himself, 'Was there ever a "game" fisherman who after a fishless week gave a damn about the birds and flowers, the view, or anything else?' – none I know.

A key to being a successful sea-trouter is being honest about what you want to get out of angling; setting some goals; and then keeping track of your progress toward attaining them. If you are a newcomer to sea-trouting, catching a

OPPOSITE: Half-frozen angler (yours truly) with a fully-frozen four-pounder (2kg) from icy February tailwaters. A deep-drifted Salmo all-rounder did the trick again!

sea trout in a season is a reasonable first goal on many waters. Once you've attained that, it's only natural to raise the bar to higher catch rates. But it's important also to be realistic. Setting too high expectations only leads to disappointment and a lot less enjoyment. What's reasonable will vary from angler to angler, water to water, season to season and method to method.

First, if you are serious about building skills as a sea-trouter you'll want to find out what the local standards are and use these as benchmarks. On some rivers, like the one I frequent, if you come home with a fish every time you go out, you are way above the average and you can pride yourself in doing well. On other rivers the standard is higher, on others lower. Some of this will be depend on the general level of skill and experience among local anglers, some of it on the numbers of fish available, some of it on the state of the water over time.

On the Manasquan River in New Jersey, for example, where sea trout and sea-trout angling have only been around since 1997, the catch rate is still very low. According to one published report, the feeling is: 'You have to put in a lot of time. If you get a bite that's a good day, if you hook one that's a great day, if you land one that's an unbelievable day.' For Mark Boriek Principal Fisheries Biologist for New Jersey, 'One fish every 24 hours is about the norm – taken over a season.' Manasquan anglers have set their performance goals accordingly. They know what to expect and have a good idea how well they are doing relative to the pack.[63]

What's a good catch can also vary from year to year on the same water. Harris and Morgan

reported catches for the Burrishoale Fishery between 1962 and 1984.[64] The average catch rate over the whole 22-year period was 0.81 fish per rod-day. But it varied from as high as 2 fish per rod-day in 1966 to as low as 0.3 per rod-day in 1984. So an angler that took a fish every time out in 1966 wasn't performing as well as one who nailed a fish every other time out in 1984. What is skilful angling is always relative.

RIGHT: 7½lb (3.4kg) sea trout.

Some anglers go for size. While I'm a small-fish enthusiast myself, I can understand the draw of scoring a lunker. On my waters you can brag about any fish over 10lb (4.5kg). On some Danish beats you won't raise an eyebrow if its under twenty (9kg)! If you are a trophy hunter find out what 'big' is where you fish.

Some anglers aim at catching fish under challenging conditions. That's what got me hooked on ice-water fishing. My cold-water catch record is a five-pounder from below freezing tailwaters.

Others go for catching fish on lures they've designed themselves. I'll admit to being addicted to that challenge too. I'd probably catch a lot more fish than I do if I stuck to using only tried- and-true lures but I'm a helpless experimenter. I usually spend a good part of my water-time tossing out lures I've made from this or that, including tin-cans, silverware, plastic soap bottles, Christmas-tree ornaments, sheet metals, you name it. For me, catching one nice fish on a home-made lure is better than catching two on a store-bought one.

How about friendly competition? Nothing wrong with that either. Sea-trout angling is after all a sport. It's only natural to want to keep score and try to outdo your cronies from time to time. If there ever was an angler who didn't relish taking fish when everybody else was drawing blanks, then I never met one.

Final Thoughts

Any tactical guide to angling has its limitations. This one is no different. Sea-trout behaviour is very complex. There is a lot we know and a lot we still don't. Distribution and migration patterns are two areas where we have only a general picture: even the experts can't really predict which waters will definitely carry sea trout or when. Like I said – too many variables. That's why the first tactical move every sea-trouter should make is to tap into local knowledge. Talk to experts at the nearest management office. Get in touch with members of the local sport fishing club. Hang around the tackle shops. These are the local nerve-centres for information and tips. Ask which waters hold sea trout and when. Ask which are the best lures to use and how they should be fished. Inform yourself on the regulations covering sea trout fishing, e.g. open seasons, permit requirements, size-limits and so on.

Following local advice and customs will get you fishing on waters you know hold sea trout and using methods you know have a decent chance of working. It won't make you a expert but it will get you started in bringing home fish. If you want to do even better than that and catch fish more consistently under a range of different conditions, even when other anglers fail, then you will need to work at it. I hope this manual will help. Tight lines!

ENDNOTES

1. The sea trout also goes by other names depending on location such as sewin, white trout and salmon trout.

2. The meagre history of writing on spin-fishing for sea trout can be traced through the following readings: Bluett (1948), Dawson (1948), Clapham (1950), Brennand (1951), Holiday (1960), McClaren (1963), Scott (1969), Falkus (1983), Jarrams (1987), Harris and Morgan (1989), Bingham (1998). These books focus mainly on fly-angling but also contain sections or chapters on spin-fishing.

3. Falkus (1983), Jarrams (1987), Harris and Morgan (1989) and Bingham (1998) contain excellent and readable sections on the basic biology, life history and distribution of sea trout in Great Britain. You can also find useful information on a web-site called *Fish Base*.

4. I've based my estimate of the optimal temperature range for sea trout from published figures for brown trout and trout generally, see: Taylor *et al.* (1996); Elliott and Hurley (2001); and Ojanguren *et al.* (2001).

5. I've gathered a lot on the ecology of the sea trout from a Swedish study by Degerman *et al.* (2001: 68).

6. See Degerman *et al.* (2001: 70) and Jardine *et al.* (2005).

7. Promille (parts per thousand) is the salt concentration level in water.

8. A study by Knutsen *et al.* (2004) reported that both young and mature sea trout spend entire winters in the salty (20–30promille) north sea off Norway's southern coast in waters ranging from 40 to 50°F (4–10°C). How widespread this is isn't yet known.

9. These figures come from the *European Federation of Sport Angling* web site and Degerman *et al.* (2001: 74).

10. See Paul Smith (2000).

11. See Harris and Morgan (1989: 13).

12. It is a common understanding that spawning sea trout, like salmon, do not hunt or feed actively while in fresh water. The fact is, when you examine the stomach contents of spawning fish you don't find much, compared to sea trout taken in the sea. A much cited study by Nall of fly-caught fish, mostly young fish (finnock or whitling) from Loch Maree in Scotland, found that 62 per cent contained little or no food. A later study by Graeme Harris of sea trout (about half whitling) from the river Afon Dyfi in Wales found little or no food in 98 per cent of the stomachs examined (Harris and Morgan 1989: 20). Hugh Falkus examined the stomachs of 300 fish caught on his stretch of river and reported only five items: 'three fly larvae; one caterpillar, and the remains of an unidentified creepy-

crawly. No fish contained for more than one item.' (1983: 41).

But the picture is a little more complex than this. Here's the current consensus:

Most mature spawning sea trout do not hunt actively when spawning. Instead they live off fat stored up during marine life and devote all energy toward spawning activities. At the same time, some small percentage, perhaps up to 20 per cent, do occasionally take food items that become available.

Young spawning fish, called finnock, may not spawn and may continue to feed in fresh water.

The likelihood that a sea trout will feed decreases as it gets closer to its spawning grounds.

Spawning females eat more than spawning males while in fresh water, according to a study of sea trout in six English rivers by Elliot (1997).

13. Studies on salmon suggest fasting in mature fish is a form of anorexia (e.g. Kadri *et al.* 1997). I wonder if it shows up as an aversion to swallowing food, not necessarily to pursuing it. That would help explain why fish we catch are usually empty of food, even though we know they take prey and lures sometimes.

14. Dave Wallbridge (2006) explains this nicely. In one study Grosman and Rosenfeld recorded the explosive strike reactions of juvenile rainbows to small floating mealworms (Barrett *et al.* 1992).

15. See Raimchen (1991).

16. Well-known salmon-troller Dick Pool, reports that salmon will miss a lure two or

three times before actually locking on. In one film, a fish hit the lure twenty-two times before getting hooked on the twenty-third! He also filmed fish that followed up bouts of repeatedly attacking and missing prey by following them at a slower speed, sometimes for long distances, before eventually grabbing them by the tail. It's uncertain whether sea trout behave exactly like this but anglers' experiences with repeated misses and followed lures seem to say they might.

17. L'Abee-Lund *et al.* (1996) report that trout don't normally swallow large or spiny prey fish like stickleback, all in one go. Instead, they stun or kill them first, usually by grabbing the tail. Once immobilized, they turn it around in their mouth or swim around and suck it in head first. According to Raimchen (1991) trout will swallow prey tail first if its diameter is less than one half the gape of a trout's mouth.

18. The fascinating history of the spoon-lure was written up by Thompson (1979) and summarized by Bill Herzog (1993).

19. See Degerman *et al.* (2001); Keeley and Grant (2001: fig. 3).

20. One survey of tagged sea trout in the Grenaekur River in Iceland by Sturlaugsson and Johannsson (1996) showed that a little over 50 per cent were young fish under 15½in (<40cm); about 35 per cent were good size fish in the 15½–23in (40–60 cm) range; and the rest, about 12 per cent, were lunkers over 23in (>60 cm). Degerman *et al.* (2001: table 20) report similar figures.

21. Good reads on salmonid vision can be found in: Douglas and Djamoz. (1990), Bryan (2002), Garth (2006), Wallbridge (2006).

22. Bernie Taylor discusses this thoroughly in

his book *Big Trout* (2002). A video study by Vogel and Beauchamp (1999) looked at the reaction distances (size of strike zone) of adult lake trout (char) to large prey fish at different light levels ranging from midday (100lx) to night time (0.17lx). As light died down to night-time levels reaction distances shrunk also, by about 75 per cent or to about 10in (25cm). However, greatest reaction distances, about 39in (100cm) on average, were not under full daylight conditions, but at light levels closer to those experienced in early dusk, late dawn, or under a darkly clouded sky (17.8lx).

23. I found the following helpful: Lumb (no date), Frederick (2001), Gibbs (2001), Aprill (2003); also the section on colour penetration in Taylor (2002).

24. See Herzog (1993).

25. Bash *et al.* (2001) summarize the evidence that salmonids prefer slightly to moderately turbid water for foraging, which seems to represent a trade-off between the predation risk of foraging in clear water and food demands.

26. See Swena and Hartman (2001).

27. This is because suspended particles in the water scatter or diffuse the shorter wave-length colours – the blues and greens – more quickly than the longer wave-length colours – reds, oranges and yellows.

28. The mechanism of trout colour-sensitivity shifts is not well understood but current research seems to show that temperature is the key. Some studies show that trout become more red-sensitive when the water is below *c.* 6°C, and more blue-sensitive when it's above 60°F (15°C) (Allen and McFarland 1973, Cristy 1976, Tsin and Beatty 1977). In one study, Muntz and Mouat (1984) documented these seasonal

changes in colour-sensitivity among fish in Scottish lochs.

The actual chemistry behind all this is beyond me. As I understand it, it's the visual pigments found in the fish's retina that absorb colours of different wave-lengths more or less. Visual pigments are formed by linking a protein (an opsin) to a vitamin A-1 or A-2, which together form either rhodopsin or porphyropsin. Porphyropsin, which is found in freshwater fish, shallow water marine fish and certain frogs, absorbs at longer wave-lengths: yellow–orange–red spectrum. Rhodopsin found in most marine fishes absorbs shorter wave-length colours in the blue–green range. This is also the chemical that allows night-vision, and is extremely sensitive to light.

29. See Ginetz and Larkin (1973).

30. See Henderson and Northcote (1985).

31. See Semler (1971).

32. See Taylor (2002).

33. See Wallbridge (2006) and Taylor (2002).

34. See Ulnits (1997).

35 See Harris and Morgan (1989: 324).

36. See Falkus (1983: 72).

37. PowerBait and Gulp, both made by Berkeley, are probably the most widely used power baits.

38. Suzanne Ayvazian, PhD. Research Scientist, Western Australian Marine Research Laboratories, reports that, 'One study reported 41.9 per cent of ... salmon hooked on treble hooks were lost compared to 33.3 per cent for single hooks. However

this level of difference did not produce a significant result.' Robert B. DuBois, Research Scientist, EIM, Kurt E. Kuklinski, Fishery Research Biologist, Fisheries Research Lab, Norman, Oklahoma and Rishard R. Dubielzig, Veternary Educator UW-Madison School of Veterinary Medicine, did research on treble versus single hook losses with wild trout from the Bois Brule River using Mepps spinners and reported that 'trebles hooked and held more trout than single hooks'.

39. Another alternative is to buy spoon components and assemble them yourself. It's not as cheap as making from scratch, but still way below retail. Mail-order is the best way to go. For a start try Real Pro's SportFishing, PO Box 17, Hepworth, ON N0H 1P0 and Stamina Quality Components, 8401 73rd Ave. N, Unit 40, Brooklyn Park, MN, 55428. Surf the web to find others. Some companies also sell components for assembling spinners.

40. Vogel and Beachamp's (1998 and 1999) video-tape studies showed that under ideal water and light conditions adult lake trout (char) struck large prey fish (rainbow and cutthroat trout, from 2 to 5½in (5.5–13.9cm)) when they were inside of about 6ft (2m), on average about 3ft (1m).

41. Newcombe (2003) illustrated the relationship between turbidity and reaction distance based on data pooled from brook, lake and rainbow trout. Rosetta (2004) summarizes research findings on the effects of turbidity on fish behaviour including reaction distance.

42. NTU is a standard unit for measuring the amount of suspended solids contained in water. The greater the amount of total suspended solids, the murkier the water appears and the higher the NTU reading.

43. Sambilay (1990) measured burst speeds of 7ft/s (2.4m/s) for a 9in (24cm) sea trout and 11ft/s (3.3m/s) for a 15in (38cm) sea trout.

44. According to David Croft (2000) sea-trout ladders are designed to assume a maximum burst speed of just over 5ft/s (1.6m/s) in 42°F (5°C) water, or about half the maximum burst speed in ideal water temperatures.

45. See Scott (1969: 182).

46. See Blomqvist (2005).

47. See Rychnovsky (1998).

48. See Young. (2005).

49. Harris and Morgan (1989) give a full account on pp. 303 and 304 (fig. 75).

50. See Falkus (1983: 33), and Taylor (2002: 65–66).

51. Due to the mysteries of nature, water actually reaches its greatest density at 40°F (4°C), which means when it gets colder than this, or even freezes, it gets lighter and floats. This strange phenomenon means that in freezing temperatures, the water can actually be a little bit warmer at the bottom.

52. Falkus (1983) believed this was due to the sea trout's sensitivity to even subtle fluctuations in the amount of dissolved oxygen in the water. Apart from water temperature, atmospheric or barometric pressure effects how much oxygen is in the water and so available to fish: when pressure is increasing, usually in clearing weather, more oxygen is dissolved and available, so fish are comfortable, alert and willing to take. Conversely, when it is falling, usually before precipitation, oxygen is driven off,

slightly less is available, so fish are less comfortable, less alert and consequently less inclined to respond to a lure's stimulus. This seems to make sense given what we know about sea-trout physiology, and is probably why many sea-trouters say fishing is rarely good on a 'falling glass' and best on a 'rising glass'.

53. See: Heggenes *et al.* (1993), Jobling *et al.* (1998), Bremset (2000), Alanära *et al.* (2001), Harwood *et al.* (2002).

54. Finnock is the name for young sea trout that make early 'spawning' runs after one summer at sea and they are mostly males. These young fish go by many other local names including herling, whitling, peale, school peal, sprod, smelt, scurff and truff, depending on location. According to Harris and Morgan (1989), on some rivers, finnock account for 80 per cent of the running fish, on others fewer than 1 per cent.

55. Chasing and tail-biting are common sights around the spawning redds. There is now evidence from a study of spawning brown trout by Broberg *et al.* (2000) that 2–3in-long sexually mature parr trout are often attacked and seriously injured by larger adult trout. No reason to think spawning sea-trout behave any differently as the redds, nor why a spoon of a similar size shouldn't elicit a similar attack!

56. See Raleigh *et al.* (1986).

57. According to Degerman *et al.* (2001: 7) sea trout have limited ability to get past large obstacles when water temperature is below around 47°F (8°C).

58. Windell *et al.* (1976) study of rainbow trout compared evacuation rates for digested worms at different water temperatures from 42 to 68°F (5–20°C). As water got warmer evacuation rates increased. So, at 42°F (5°C) it took 58.5h to fully digest and evacuate worms, while at 68°F (20°C) it only took only 16.4h.

59. A study by Koskela *et al.* (1997) showed that while feeding rate is initially greatly reduced when the water drops below 44°F (6°C), after a few weeks of acclimatization trout and salmon will begin to increase feeding rate again.

60. According to Taylor *et al.* (1996) power-dams warm water by 4°F (2°C) on average during winter and cool it by 10°F (6°C) on average in summer.

61. Baltic coast anglers Steen Ulnits, Martin Joergensen, Claus Eriksen and Tord Andreasson maintain informative web sites with English-language pages worth taking a look at. Start with: www.seatrout.dk

62. Sturlaugsson and Johannsson's (1996) study of radio-tagged sea trout from the River Grenaekur in SE Norway showed that even in the open sea, sea trout spent most of their time in the upper 5m (16ft). That's where salinity was lowest (*c.* 34promille) and temperature highest (47–50°F or 8–10°C). Although some dives down to 85ft (26m) were also recorded.

63. New Jersey State's Fish, Game and Wildlife web-pages describe the history and catch records for sea trout introduced in the Manasqua drainage (www.state.nj.us/dep/fgw).

64. See Harris and Morgan (1989: fig. 81).

BIBLIOGRAPHY

Alanärä A., Burns M.D., and Metcalfe N.B. 'Intraspecific resource partitioning in brown trout: the temporal distribution of foraging is determined by social rank', *Journal of Animal Ecology* (Vol. 70, No. 6, 2001, pp. 980–986).

Allen, D. M. and McFarland, W. N., 'Effect of temperature on rhodopsin-porphyropsin ratios in a fish', *Vision Research* (Vol. 13, 1973, pp. 1303–1309).

Aprill, D., 'Certain colors are really fishy', *Plattsburgh (NY) Press-Republican*, 7-13-03.

Andreasson, T., 'Spinnfiske efter Havsöring på kusten', *Skanska kustfiskeklubben* (2005). (http://goto.glocalnet.net/skanskakustfiskeklubben/teknik/spinnfis.htm)

Barrett, J. D; Grossman, G. D. and Risenfeld, J., 'Turbidity induced changes on reaction distance in rainbow trout', *Transactions of the American Fisheries Society* (Vol. 121, 1992, pp. 437–443).

Bash, J., C. Berman and Balton, S., 'Effects of Turbidity and Suspended Solids on Salmonids', *Centre for Streamside Studies* (University of Washington, 2001).

Bingham, C., *Sea Trout. How to Catch Them* (Swan Hill Press, Airlife Publishing Ltd, 1998).

Blomqvist, B., 'Pimpelfiske efter havsöring I bohuslan', *Sportfishing News* (2005). (www.outdoor.se/sportfishnews/)

Bluett, J., *Sea Trout and Occasional Salmon* (Cassell and Co. Ltd, 1948).

Bremset, G., 'Seasonal and diet changes in behaviour, microhabitat use and preferences by young pool-dwelling Atlantic salmon, *Salmo salar*, and brown trout, *Salmo trutta*', *Environment and Biology of Fishes* (Vol. 59, No. 2, 2000, pp. 163–179).

Brennand, G., *The Fisherman's Handbook: Trout, Salmon and Sea Trout, with Notes on Coarse Fishing* (Ward Lock and Co. Ltd, 1951).

Broberg, M. M., Nielsen, E. E. and C. Dieperink, C., 'Incidence of physical injury of mature male parr in a natural population of brown trout', *Journal of Fish Biology* (Vol. 57, No. 6, 2000, pp. 1610–1612).

Bryan, J., 'Trout Eyeballs, Fours Cones, and the Black Light Elvis' (www.outdoors.net, 2002).

Clapham, R., *Fishing for Sea Trout in Tidal Waters* (Oliver and Boyd, 1950).

Cristy M., 'Effects of temperature and light intensity on the visual pigments of rainbow trout', *Vision Research* (Vol. 16, No. 11, 1976, pp. 1225–1228).

Croft, D. 'Fish Passage. Fish Pass Ladder Design' (Croft Consultants, 2000).

Dawson, K., *Modern Salmon and Sea Trout Fishing* (Herbert Jenkins, Ltd, 1948).

Degerman, E., and Sers, B., *Havsöringens ekologi* (Fiskeverket Informerar, 2001).

Douglas R. H. and. Djamoz, M.B.A., *The Visual System of Fish* (Chapman and Hall, 1990).

Elliott J.M., 'Stomach contents of adult sea trout caught in six English rivers', *Journal of Fish Biology* (Vol. 50, No. 5, 1997, pp. 1129–1132).

Elliott J. M. and Hurley M. A., 'Modelling growth of brown trout, *Salmo trutta*, in terms of weight and energy units', *Freshwater Biology* (Vol. 46, 2001, pp. 679–692).

Falkus, H., *Sea Trout Fishing* (H.F. and G. Witherby Ltd, 1983).

Frederick, L., *How to select lure colours for successful fishing* (Report available on request to University of Wisconsin Sea Grant Institute, 2001).

Gammon, C., *Sea Trout* (Osprey Publishing Ltd, 1974).

Garth, M., 'Colour in the Fishes Eyes' (web publication, 2006). (www.sextloops.com/articles/whatsalmonidsee.shtml)

Gibbs, J., 'Visionary Angling' (web publication, 2001). (www.outdoorlife.com)

Ginetz, R. M. and Larkin, P. A., 'Choice of colours of food items by rainbow trout (*Salmo gairdnerii*)', *Journal of Fisheries Research Board of Canada* (Vol. 30, 1973, pp.229–234).

Harwood, A. J., Metcalfe, N.B., Armstrong, J.D. and Griffiths, S.W., 'Spatial and temporal effects of interspecific competition between Atlantic salmon (*Salmo salar*) and brown trout (*Salmo trutta*) in winter', *Canadian Journal of Fisheries and Aquatic Science* (Vol. 58, No. 6, 2001, pp. 1133–1140).

Harris, G. and Morgan, M., *Successful Sea Trout Angling* (Coch-Y-Bondu Books, 1989).

Heggenes, J. O., Krog, M., Lindas, O.R., Dokk, J.G. and Bremmes, T., 'Homeostatic behavioral responses in the changing environment: brown trout (*salmo trutta*) become nocturnal during winter', *Journal of Animal Ecology* (Vol. 62, 1993, pp. 295–308).

Henderson, M. A. and Northcote, T. G., 'Visual prey detection and foraging in sympatric cutthroat trout (*Salmo clarki clarki*) and Dolly Varden (*Salvelinus malma*)', *Canadian Journal of Fisheries and Aquatic Sciences* (Vol. 42, 1985, pp. 785–94).

Johansson, J., *Havsöringsfiske* (Bokforlaget Settern, 1988).

Kadri, S., Thorpe, J.E. and Metcalfe, N.B., 'Anorexia in one-sea-winter Atlantic salmon (Salmo salar) during summer, associated with sexual maturation', *Aquaculture* (Vol. 151, No. 1, 1997, pp. 405–409).

Keeley, E. and Grant, J., 'Prey Size of salmonid fishes in streams, lakes, and oceans', *Canadian Journal of Aquatic Sciences* (Vol. 58, 2001, pp. 1122–1132).

Knutsen, J.A., Knutsen, H., Olsen, E.M. and Jonsson, B., 'Marine feeding of anadromous Salmo trutta during winter', *Journal of Fish Biology* (Vol. 64, 2004, pp. 89–99).

Koskela, J., Pirhonen, J. and Jobling, M., 'Variations in feed intake and growth of Baltic salmon and brown trout exposed to continuous light at constant low temperature', *Journal of Fish Biology* (Vol. 50, No. 4, 1997, p. 837).

L'Abee-Lund J. H., Aass P. and Saegrov, H., 'Prey orientation in piscivorous brown trout', *Journal of Fish Biology* (Vol. 48, No. 5, 1996, pp. 871–877).

Lumb, D., 'Lure Fishing in coloured water' (Muskie Central, no date). (www.muskiecentral.com)

McClaren, C.C., *The Art of Sea Trout Fishing* (Oliver and Boyd Ltd, 1963).

Muntz, W. R. A. and Mouat, G. S. V., 'Annual variations in the visual pigments of brown trout inhabiting lochs providing different light environments', *Vision Research* (Vol. 24, No. 11, 1984, pp. 1575–1580).

Newcombe, C. *Impact Assessment Model for Clear Water Fishes Exposed to Excessively Cloudy Water.* (American Water Resources Association, 2003).

Ojanguren, A. F., Felipe, G., Reyes-Gavila, N. and Brana, F., 'Thermal sensitivity of growth, food intake and activity of juvenile brown trout', *Journal of Thermal Biology* (Vol. 26, 2001, pp. 165–170).

Pool, D. 'Salmon Fishing Techniques' (web publication, no date). (www.protroll.com/salmon)

Raleigh, R. F., Zuckerman, L.D. and Nelson, P.C., 'Habitat suitability index models and instream flow suitability curves: brown trout', *Biological Report* (Vol. 82, No 10, 1986, National Ecology Center, Division of Wildlife and Contaminant Research, Research and Development, Fish and Wildlife Service, US Department of the Interior, Washington, DC).

Raimchen, T.E., 'Trout foraging failures and the evolution of body size in sticklebacks', *Copeia* (Vol. 1991, No. 4, 13 Dec 1991, pp. 1098–1104)

Rosetta, T., *Technical Basis for revising turbidity criteria.* (Draft manuscript. Water Quality Division, The Oregon Department of Environmental Quality, 2004).

Rychnovsky, R., 1998, *The Troller's Handbook for all American Fish Species* (Frank Amato Publications, Inc. 1998).

Sambiley, V.C., Jnr, 'Interrelationships between swimming speed, caudal fin aspect ratio and body length in fishes', *Fishbyte* (Vol. 8, No. 3. 1990, pp. 16–20).

Scott, J., *Seatrout Fishing* (Seely, Service and Co. Ltd, 1969).

Semler, D., 'Some aspects of adaptation in a polymorphism for breeding colours in the threespine stickleback' (*Gasterosteus aculeatus*), *Journal of Zoology* (Vol. 165, 971, pp. 291–302).

Smith, P., 'Sea-run brown trout fishing in Newfoundland. Parts 1 and 2' (*Our Man In Canada, Fly-anglers on Line,* 2000). (www.flyanglersonline.com/features/canada/can111.html)

Sturlaugsson, J. and Johannsson, M., *Migratory pattern of wild sea trout* (salmo trutta L.) *in SE-Iceland recorded by data storage tags* (International Council for the Exploration of the Sea. C. M. 1996/M:5).

Ström, M., 'Om havsöring' (West Coast Charters in Swedish Westcoast Archipelago, 2005). (www.sportfiske.org/havsoring.html)

Sweka, J. A. and Hartman, K.J., 'Effects of turbidity on prey consumption and growth in brook trout and implications for bioenergetics modeling', *Canadian Journal of Fisheries and Aquatic Sciences* (Vol. 58, 2001, pp. 386–393).

Taylor, B., *Big Trout. How and Where to Target Trophies* (The Lyons Press, 2002).

Taylor, S., Egginton, S. and Taylor, E., 'Seasonal temperature acclimatisation of rainbow trout: cardiovascular and morphometric influences on maximal sustainable exercise level', *Journal of Experimental Biology* (Vol. 199, Issue 4, 1996, pp. 835–845).

Thompson, H., *The Spooners* (Special publication of the Eppinger Manufacturing Co, 1979)

Tsin, A.T. and Beatty, D.D., 'Visual pigment changes in rainbow trout in response to temperature', *Science* (Vol. 95, No. 4284, 1977, pp. 1358–1360).

Ulnits, S. 1997. 'Steen Ulnits' home page' (1997). (www.ulnits.dk)

Vogel, J. L. and Beauchamp, D. A., 'Effects of light, prey size, and turbidity on reaction distances of lake trout (*Salvelinus namaycush*) to salmonid prey', *Canadian Journal of Fisheries and Aquatic Sciences* (Vol. 56, No. 7, 1999, pp. 1293–1297).

Vogel, J. L. and Beauchamp, D. A., *Reaction Distances of Salmonids, Scaled to Detection Distances of SCUBA Divers, for Use in a General Piscivore Foraging Model* (unpublished manuscript, 1998).

Wallbridge, D., 'Fish vision – and the Salmonids' (web publication, 2006). (www.sextloops.com/articles/whatsalmonidsee.shtml)

Windell, J. T., Kitchell, J. F., Norris, D. O. and Foltz, J. W., 'Temperature and rate of gastric evacuation by rainbow trout, *Salmo gairdneri*', *Transactions of the American Fisheries Society* (Vol. 105, 1976, pp. 712–717).

Young, H., 'Trolling – the 'old school' way' (web publication, 2005). (www.trollingthe scottishlochs.co.uk)

INDEX